THE LONG WAR ON IRAN

The United States and Iran have been locked in a decades-long standoff, driven by missteps, misunderstandings, and conflicting ambitions. This book, from a prominent Iranian authority, delves into the complex dynamics behind this ongoing conflict. It sheds light on why American policies have repeatedly failed to understand the true nature of Iran's transformations and its role in the Middle East.

Drawing on two decades of political analysis, Ghamari explores the history of US intervention in the region, focusing on the enduring sanctions imposed on Iran and the persistent perception of the Islamic Republic as a major obstacle to American power. Despite the repressive policies of the state, Iran has remained a vibrant society with active intellectual, cultural, and social justice movements. The book examines these internal changes and shifts in Iranian politics.

By challenging the conventional *image* of Iran as a totalitarian regime, Ghamari urges readers to appreciate the country's diverse society and complex political landscape. It calls for a re-evaluation of how the US engages with Iran, advocating for a more informed, nuanced approach to Middle East diplomacy. At a critical moment when US policy is being reshaped, *The Long War on Iran* is a timely reminder that, if the US fails to acknowledge Iran's transformations, both nations will continue to face new events—and the same old questions.

THE LONG WAR ON IRAN

New Events Old Questions

BEHROOZ GHAMARI

O/R
OR Books
New York • London

Published by OR Books, New York and London

Visit our website at www.orbooks.com

All rights information: rights@orbooks.com

First printing 2026

The manufacturer's authorised representative in the EU for product safety is Authorised Rep Compliance Ltd, 71 Lower Baggot Street, Dublin D02 P593 Ireland (www.arccompliance.com)

Typeset by Lapiz Digital. Printed by BookMobile, USA, and CPI, UK.

paperback ISBN 978-1-68219-671-7• ebook ISBN 978-1-68219-672-4

Cover by: Mahdi Molaee. Tehran Grand Bazaar, October 2022. Unsplash License

CONTENTS

SECTION III
AMERICAN POLITICS

SECTION IV
DISSENT AND PROTEST IN IRAN

SECTION V
MUSLIM VOICES AND THE MEDIA

INTRODUCTION

The Long War on Iran

Sanctions, Assassinations, and Bombs

In February 1984, I was a death row prisoner at Evin Prison in Tehran when Saddam Hussein began his first systematic campaign of bombardment of Iranian cities. At the time, I was alone in an infirmary cell, weak with advanced lymphoma. The ward was particularly quiet. Occasionally, the distant moaning of a prisoner in another cell broke the stabbing silence of the infirmary. The roaring sound of missiles shaking the city further complicated the purgatory of waiting for execution, while fading from my untreated cancer.

Every evening for almost two weeks, I sat on my bed trying to devise a plan for when the missiles hit the prison. Do I run toward the nearest exit? What if the guards shoot indiscriminately at escaping prisoners? Do I crawl under my bed to save myself from the debris? Do I just lie calmly on my bed and accept the inevitable?

One evening, a guard who noticed my anxiety assured me that the missiles were not going to hit the prison. "If they do, we all go together, that's the only thing we have in common," he said mockingly. Usually, he was not very chatty. He was in charge of tending to a deep wound on my neck and seldom uttered a word as he changed its bandage every other day. He did his job reluctantly and made sure that I knew of his ambivalence by reminding me that I was going to be executed anyway—*why bother.*

In a twisted way, the bombings forced both of us to transcend our positions: the possibility of being buried under the same wreckage could bring fleeting moments of solidarity. He told me about his tours of the warfront in the south and how he never got used to sseeing the torn-apart bodies of those who fought to fend off the Iraqi aggression. He held back the flow of sorrow with a rattled smile, as he named among those, "my younger brother, who's now in the heavens." He quickly became conscious of the theater of the absurd we shared. Here were the confessions of a prison guard to a death row prisoner accused of the plot to overthrow the very government he was guarding, not only against the domestic insurgents, but also against foreign invasion.

I was arrested three years earlier for membership in a radical Marxist organization that intended to topple the Islamic Republic. I was tried and sentenced to death four months after my arrest and had been waiting since for the sentence to be carried out. After a year on death row, I developed cancer, which had remained untreated for several months until it advanced to, what the prison officials believed, a terminal stage.

After the initial shock of hearing and feeling the impact of the Iraqi bombs in the city, I felt a deep sense of resignation. I had no doubt that I would die soon, either from cancer or by firing squad. My acquiescence, lying in bed without any appearance of outrage, was an expression of futility, nothing more. But it gave the guards the impression that I welcomed Hussein's attacks, and that a possible destruction of Evin prison could offer me a chance to survive. Far from it, I knew at the time that Hussein's aggression was primarily an attempt to take advantage of the instability after the revolution to expand the Iraqi territories and appropriate Iranian oil fields. Although my other comrades and I were on the losing side of the postrevolutionary power struggle, I remained faithful to the ideals of the revolution and the emancipatory politics that gave rise to it.

Iraqi forces had invaded a large swath of southwest Iran in a surprise attack at the end of the summer of 1980. After two years of bloody battle, the Iranian side regained control of its territory. Suffering crushing losses on the war fronts, Hussein began to attack major cities, like Tehran, to disrupt Iranian morale and compel the people to overthrow their own government in order to end the war. In two weeks, from February 7 to February 22, 1984, Iraqi bombs and missiles killed more than 4,700 and wounded over 20,000 civilians. Iran retaliated in kind.

At the time, Iraq was a client state of the Soviet Union. The Soviets were the main supplier of arms and munition to Iraq, their air raids were carried out with Soviet-made jet fighters. Although the Cold War was still at its height, the US and other NATO members saw in the Iraqi aggression an opportunity to contain the Iranian revolution and a chance for lucrative arms deals. The French offered Saddam Hussein their Mirage-F1 fighter jets to combat Iranian F-14 Tomcats. German companies transferred tons of material for use in chemical weapons that Hussein deployed against civilians using US-made Bell helicopters. In addition to intelligence sharing, the Reagan administration provided the Iraqi regime with billions of dollars of economic aid, preventing the total collapse of their economy.

My worst fear of being buried under Evin prison rubble did not materialize. Evin was not bombed at that time. After eight years and hundreds of thousands of casualties on both sides, millions of people displaced, economies in ruins, in 1988, a peace treaty was signed between Iran and Iraq. The war ended but the US project of containing Iran and remapping the Middle East persisted. After the collapse of the Soviet Union in 1991, American patience for any form of challenge to its hegemony in the emerging unipolar world order dwindled.

The response to the 9/11 attacks demonstrated how far Washington would go to display its unmatched military might and its willingness to execute disproportionate power against perceived enemies. Iran remained on top of the target list. One week before the invasion of Iraq in March 2003, I was invited to Washington DC for a workshop on Iran policy. Now a professor of sociology, I thought that the purpose of the workshop was to find a way to avoid the spread of war to Iran. But the meeting with a small group of the State Department and Congressional staff was about how fast the US forces could march to Tehran after conquering Baghdad. This was the time that Iran was experiencing a period of Thermidorian reaction to the 'reign of terror' of the 1980s when thousands were executed and hundreds of thousands were imprisoned or exiled. The reformist government of President Khatami had come to power with two mantras; "dialouge of civilizations," a candid antidote to Samuel Huntington's infamous *Clash of Civilizations,* and "Iran for Iranians" that Washington was not ready to hear. The White House and the entire neoconservative political class were intoxicated with the fantasy of "Boys go to Baghdad, real men go to Tehran."

The Islamic Republic learned quickly that, in addition to a repressive rule, its existence depended on creating a ring of fire around its borders as a deterrent to the American and Israeli ambitions to redraw the map of the region. More than evidence of its expansionist project, the Islamic Republic's investment in the Lebanese Hezbollah, supporting the Assad regime in Syria, and defending the Palestinian cause, had to do with its own security. That is not to say that they did not have ideological convictions against US hegemony and Israel's largely unchecked reign in the region. But, as Henry Precht, the former director of the Iran desk at the State Department, aptly observed in 1988, what motivates the Islamic Republic is "political and economic independence at home, not dominion abroad."

On June 23, 2025, amid the horrors of another imposed war on Iran, I had the uncanny experience of watching the news from my home in New York City when the Israeli forces bombed Evin prison in northern Tehran. What I feared more than forty years ago had finally happened. How perplexing that I felt that my home was attacked. That visceral reaction stayed with me for several days. As the news continued to come out, we learned that seventy-nine people were killed, most of whom were prison employees, including social workers and legal staff, as well as many people who were there to visit their imprisoned loved ones. The news also came out that rather than running away, many prisoners rushed toward where the bombs had landed to rescue those under the rubble, among them, a number of interrogators, staff of the prosecutor's office, and medical staff at the infirmary. After surviving the attack, Dr. Sa'ideh Makaram, who volunteered as a physician at Evin, told the reporters that she had been half-dead, buried under the rubble. "The prisoners pulled me out and took me to a safer corner. They brought me water and wrapped my shivering body with a blanket. They immobilized my broken leg with a makeshift splint and wiped the blood off my face. They could run away, but they stayed. One of them told me that you're our sister, we would never leave you alone here."

The bombing of Evin, which is well-known for housing political prisoners, once again brought the Iranian conundrum to surface. Four decades after the Iraqi attacks, here was the regime that came to power as a result of the 1979 revolution still trying to uphold a meaningful sovereignty in a geopolitical tinderbox. The Islamic Republic has used all instruments of power to curb dissent by linking workers, women, students, ethnic, and religious minority movements in the face of belligerent foreign intervention, thus turning repression into a means of sustaining sovereignty. The foreign enemy dropping bombs on Evin complicates that calculus. It offers recognition to the plight of those voices of dissent, while at the same time, gives currency to the regime's anxieties about foreign powers' desire to instigate a regime change in Iran (see Chapter 24: Lost Muslim Voices of Dissent).

Ten days earlier, Israel had launched an unprovoked attack on Iran, assassinating top commanders of the Iranian military and launching bombs and missiles at Tehran and other major cities. They killed more than 1,000 people and wounded thousands more during a twelve day campaign aimed at destroying Iranian nuclear enrichment sites and with the ostensible expectation that, as a result of the bombing, Iranians would rise up and overthrow the Islamic Republic. After the initial blow, the government organized a massive response, showering Israeli cities with home-made missiles, some of which were able to penetrate the seemingly invincible Iron Dome.

Forty years ago, all world powers lined up in support of Saddam Hussein's aggression, but this time Israel was assigned to do, in the German Chancellor's words, "the dirty work for us in Iran." For more than thirty years, Israeli leadership had been claiming that Iran is just a few months away from making a nuclear bomb. In 1992, Benjamin Netanyahu, then a non-ranking member of the Knesset, warned that Tehran was only a few years away from acquiring a nuclear bomb, a claim that he repeated in his 1995 book, *Fighting Terrorism.* In his infamous UN General Assembly speech in September 2012, equipped with a cartoonish graph, he warned the world that Iran was on the threshold of making and deploying a nuclear bomb. "By next spring ... they will be ready to move on to the final stage."

Netanyahu at the UN General Assembly, September 2012

Israel's attack on Iran was in the making for decades (and had enjoyed several mini-rehearsals). So was the Islamic Republic's response.

Nearly since it came to power, the Islamic Republic has justified its repressive policies and the limits it imposes on civil liberties as necessary measures to check the external threats against its existence. Western observers often frame the formation of the Iranian security state as a reflection of the chronic paranoia of Ayatollah Khamenei, the Supreme Leader. They project this pathology in order to disavow their own role in generating the conditions for a securitized society. Comments such as "Ayatollah Khamenei's blind paranoia explains the ferocity of repression in Iran,"[1] "Battered by war, Tehran responds with repression and paranoia,"[2] "Ayatollah Khamenei hides in his bunker as paranoia stalks Iran,"[3] "as the US enters the war, Iranians huddle in the dark while their ruler retreats into paranoia,"[4] have been common in Western media. It seems baffling that after decades of overt and covert Israeli operations inside Iran, including sabotage, assassination, cyber-attacks, and espionage, the mainstream media characterizes the Iranian leadership as overly suspicious. Even after Israel and its allies initiated a full-blown war and issued threats to kill the Supreme Leader, boasting about their sleeper cells and how they have infiltrated the highest echelons of the state and intelligence services, the media continues to deem the securitization of society as the regime's paranoia reaching a "fever pitch."

The day before Israel's initial attack, the International Atomic Energy Agency (IAEA) called for an emergency meeting in

---

1 Jean-Pierre Filiu, *Le Monde,* January 15, 2023.

2 Bahar Makooi, *France 24,* June 26, 2025.

3 Samer al-Atrush, *Sunday Times,* June 20, 2025.

4 Rana Rahimpour, *The Observer,* June 21, 2025.

Vienna to report that Iran was in breach of its obligations under the Nonproliferation Treaty (NPT) Safeguards. Contrary to US media headlines, the IAEA report contained no new information or any evidence of Iran's noncompliance or any weaponization program. Instead, it highlighted the agency's dissatisfaction with a decades-old event. The report pointed to Iran's 2003 response to questions about the military component of its program, and the discovery of additional highly enriched particles of uranium in three sites at that time. Although Rafael Grossi, the IAEA Director, clearly stated that there was no evidence of a weaponization program and consistent monitoring had taken place in the twenty years since, he raised suspicions about Iran's transparency and good faith.

The IAEA meeting in Vienna took place after the Israeli government had already informed the US and European allies that an attack on Iran was imminent. Before the IAEA submitted its report in the meeting, the plans were drawn, the support was pledged, and the light had turned green for the Israelis to obliterate Iranian nuclear sites and vital infrastructure regardless of the substantial human toll. At the time, Iran and the US were in the middle of negotiating a new agreement on the limits and the scope of the Iranian enrichment program. The two sides had met five times in Oman and Italy. They were supposed to meet again in Oman in two days when Israel attacked Iranian cities. Like the international coalition that sustained Hussein's war of aggression, Israel launched its attack with the help of the US and its allies. A US tanker aircraft took off from a military base in Qatar to deliver aerial refueling to the Israeli jet fighters whose range would otherwise not allow them to reach Iranian targets. While the British and the Americans stockpiled billions of dollars of arms in Israel, the French helped Israel to intercept Iranian retaliatory missiles, and Jordan and Iraq were pressured to open their respective airspace to the Israelis to carry out their attacks.

Fresh in the minds of Iranians was Israel's genocide in Palestine. Bombing Iranian cities immediately evoked the images of complete destruction of Gazan cities. Iranians knew that the Israelis possess no inhibition in committing war crimes and acts of genocide. They and their American backers wanted Iranians to have the image of Gaza in their mind, of the atrocities they are capable of, and to force them to surrender unconditionally in the first few days of the assaults. They also had hoped that the attacks would instigate regime change through mobilization from below led by domestic and diasporic dissidents. Bombing Evin prison could be understood as a manifestation of the naïve fantasy of the latter option: razing the prison gates, with the masses storming Evin, carrying freed political prisoners on their shoulders, and celebrating the end of the Islamic Republic in a replay of the Fall of the Bastille.

Many Iranian dissidents in exile held the Islamic Republic responsible for the war. They ranged from those who dream of the return of the pre-revolution Pahlavi monarchy to those who hoped for a democratic transformation of the existing political order that could accommodate US interests in the region. The monarchists understand that the key issue in reclaiming Iran's position in the region is the question of sovereignty. In no uncertain terms, Reza Pahlavi, the former Shah's son, has situated himself as an ally of the US and Israel, even more so during the war. The monarchists know that the

US needs a client state in Iran and they intend to prove that they are the best alternative to fulfill that mandate.

Within Iran, the situation was not so straightforward. Many who scorn and distrust their government nonetheless see Israel clearly, and do not welcome its violent interference. How could an increasingly theocratic state in Israel, with its Biblical claim to land and statehood, along with authoritarian regimes like Egypt, the United Arab Emirates (UAE), Saudi Arabia, and other American allies in the Middle East, demand a secular-democratic Iran as the solution to the existing conflict? Those dissidents who believe that a democratic and secular Iran would ease tensions with the West fail to see how the US and its allies instrumentalize human rights and civil liberties as a means of expanding their influence around the world, while giving themselves a pass on atrocities—a fact that has become even clearer two plus years into the Gaza genocide.

The majority of Americans believe that the US is a benevolent force for good, and that it has the moral authority to lead the rest of the world toward a better future. Many Iranian dissidents subscribe to this myth, in a sharp departure from the anti-imperialist position of those who led and participated in the revolutionary movement of the 1970s. At the time, for Iranian revolutionaries, what happened in Vietnam and Cambodia, in Indonesia and East Timur, in Palestine, in Africa—from Algeria to South Africa—in Chile, Brazil, and Argentina, in Guatemala, El Salvador, and Nicaragua, and in Cuba were all relevant to their struggle against the tyranny of the Shah and his regime's proxy exercise of military might on behalf of American interests in the Middle East.

Geopolitical issues have always been integrated into the issues of social justice and civil liberties. In recent years, many domestic and diasporic critics of the Islamic Republic began to distance themselves from regional and global struggles for justice, focusing solely on the Islamic Republic's repression against its own citizens. This is not to discount cruel domestic policies of the Islamic Republic, but to link those policies to wider concerns about American expansionism and the Israeli ambitions to realize a greater Israel from the river to the sea, and that river, for maximalist Zionists, is no longer the Jordan but the Euphrates.

Iranian reformists adopted the slogan *na Ghazeh, na Lobnan, Jānam fadā-ye Iran* (Not for Gaza, not for Lebanon, my heart beats for Iran) in the early 2010s. The suggestion was that the Islamic Republic's investment in supporting what has become known as the axis of resistance, Hezbollah in Lebanon, the Assad regime in Syria, paramilitary forces in Iraq, Palestinian armed groups, and the Houthis in Yemen, drains the dwindling resources of the country to the detriment of Iranian people. The policy, they argued, places Iran at the center of regional conflicts, which in turn justifies the increasing securitization of the entire society. These critics fail to recognize that *so long as Iranian national interests remain in conflict with those of the Israelis and Americans, Iran would be demonized, regardless of the character of the state that rules the country.*

For many years, the Iranian government has argued that it supports forces who fight on the streets of Damascus, Baghdad, Beirut, and in Palestine, so that the fight will not unfold on the streets of Tehran and other Iranian cities. The Israeli attacks on Iran, after the fall of Bashar al-Assad, decapitation of Hezbollah, and the genocidal assault against Hamas and the Palestinians of Gaza, made that logic more plausible than ever. The containment of Iran and forcing the Islamic Republic to submit to the colonial interests of Western powers and their clients in the Middle East defines the master frame of US policies in the region. This has been the case since the dawn of the Revolution of 1979 which disrupted the status quo of the region with the collapse of the Pahlavi monarchy.

Mohammad Reza Shah, the second monarch of the Pahlavis, was himself an instance of the American containment policy in the Middle East. Most often, the story that is told about the US-Iran relations begins with the hostage crisis of 1979. But I came of age in Iran in the 1970s when people of my generation, and the generation before me, could not think of the US without recalling the 1953 joint CIA-MI6 coup against Mohammad Mosaddeq, the democratically elected prime minister who nationalized the oil industry. At that time, Iranians were acutely aware that they did not have any input in the management of the Anglo-Iranian oil company and no right to audit its books. Iran's revenue share from its own precious national resource was less than 20 percent. The oil workers were paid 50 cents a day with no sick time, vacation, compensation for disability, or any pension programs.

Amid rising nationalist sentiment and anti-imperialist liberation movements around the world, the Iranian prime minister believed that the demand for a fair share of the nation's natural resources would find a receptive audience, even in the US. He was mistaken. Informed by a Cold War outlook that only tyrannical regimes could impede the spread of communism, the US decided that the liberal Mosaddeq lacked the necessary backbone to run the country with the iron fist required to curb Soviet expansionism. The coup that ousted Mosaddeq in the summer of 1953 was the most consequential CIA covert operation, code-named Operation Ajax.

At the time, Iran served as one of the strongest footholds of American interests around the world. Its location in the Middle East, particularly when the settler colonial state of Israel was in its infancy, made Iran a strategic outpost that the West could not afford to lose. Mosaddeq's resolve in defending Iran's sovereignty and the nationwide popular support that backed his project forced the Shah to leave the country. With the coup, the CIA brought Mohammad Reza Shah back from Rome and reinstalled him to the throne. Under his royal tutelage, the country became a perfect client state, and in the process earned the nickname *the gendarme of the region.* He ruled Iran for another twenty-five years after the coup, years that are known in the Iranian political lexicon as the dark ages of despotism.

The mainstream media depicted the 1979 hostage crisis as story of crazy mullahs and their militant Muslim student supporters taking over the American embassy in Tehran and holding dozens hostage for 444 days. They hate us for our defense of freedom and for our democratic values. This Orwellian narrative is often depicted sarcastically by the critics who point out that the problem with the Islamic Republic is that it has put Iran near American military bases, airfields, radar and navy facilities, in Bahrain, Qatar, UAE, Jordan, Saudi Arabia, Iraq, and Kuwait, with more than 40,000 troops on the ground.

US Military Facilities in the Middle East

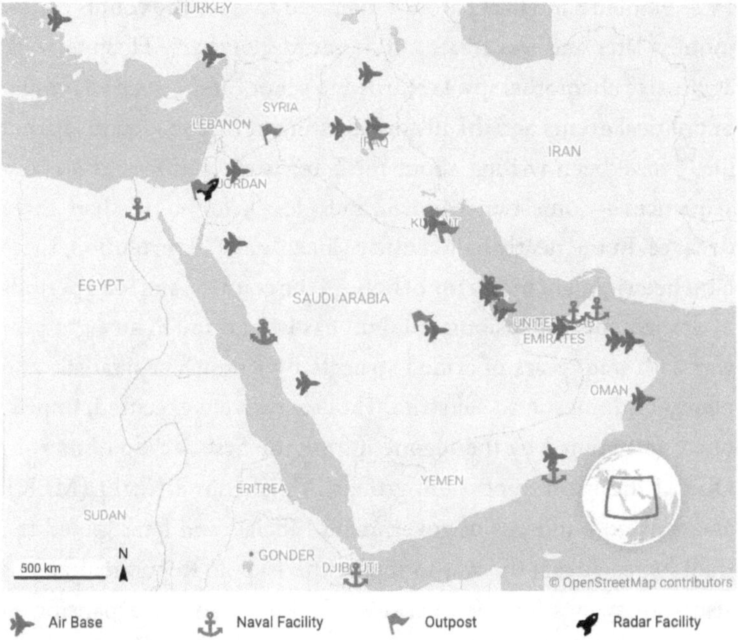

Source: American Security Project

The US-Israel attack in 2025 was about Iran's challenge to regional hegemony, the history of which goes back to the 1953 coup. There is no coincidence that Israel's unprovoked attack, with US and European support, happened amid the ongoing genocide in Palestine, and on the heels of Israel's invasion of Lebanon, and the installation of a former senior ISIS/al-Qaeda operative as the head of state in Syria. For decades, these wars, assassinations, sabotage, and cyber-attacks happened in secret and behind the public eye. Now their masks are off.

In 1985, after the High Judicial Council annulled my death sentence, I was granted a medical parole. I managed to leave the country a few months later and was treated at Stanford University Hospital with aggressive chemotherapy. I returned to school and became a scholar of political events and the historical moment that shaped my earlier life. I have been writing about the Iranian revolution and its consequences—domestic, regional, and global, for more than three decades. In the nearly half-century since the 1979 revolution, there have been jubilant moments of hope in the country, and long periods of despair and disillusionment. Iran has been through an eight-year war with Iraq, years of armed struggle by Kurdish separatists, and plenty of domestic social strife. Thousands were executed, imprisoned, or maimed by the regime during the first decade of its rule. One of the main opposition groups, Mojahedin-e Khalq (MEK), assassinated hundreds of government officials and later joined the Iraqi forces during the war to topple the Islamic Republic. Iran has also seen swings between periods of reform and the expansion of civil society, all the while sustained by a repressive state apparatus that has thus far maintained a tight grip on political power.

The US has gone through eight presidencies since Carter was ousted over his failure to return the Embassy hostages; a failure that was choreographed by the Ronald Reagan campaign team to make sure that the hostages remained in Iran until after the Presidential election of 1980. Since then, there have been periods of rapprochement, followed by increasing hostility, and a continuous series of crushing sanctions that have taken a terrible toll on the Iranians of all walks of life. We've seen a War on Terror and the labelling of Iran as an "Axis of Evil," followed by attempts to sign a nuclear agreement with Iran only to see that same agreement ripped up by another president, who now wants to strike a new deal even as he witnessed the Israeli assassination of one of the lead Iranian negotiators. All this comes after he imposed the most draconian economic sanctions in recent history on the country.

Despite major events in the past four decades, the neo-colonial power structure remains an enduring problem that continues to shape the political landscape of the Middle East. Central to the existing political order are two basic questions around which US strategic interests are articulated. These are, in alternating orders of significance, the question of Palestine, and of the Islamic Republic of Iran. Since its inception in 1979, the Islamic Republic of Iran has exercised its own sovereign power to extend its regional political authority. The enduring question of the past four decades is Iran's sovereignty, its refusal to become a client state aligned with American interests in the region. The US and its European allies instrumentalize the Islamic Republic's repressive state apparatus, its appalling violations of human rights (though arguably much less so than Western allies in the region), patriarchal legal system, and its limitations on civil liberties to justify their attempts to force Iran to submit to their demands. The fact that the most reliable allies of the Western powers in the region, i.e., Saudi Arabia and Egypt, have atrocious records of naked despotism and brutal governance, is a clear indication that the protection of human rights and dignity does not drive American interests in the region, regardless of the lip-service they are given when directed at Iran.

The genocidal war in Gaza has generated an unprecedented global condemnation of Israel; the long-term question of Palestine—of occupation and settler colonialism has remained urgent and seemingly intractable. Millions of people around the world have marched against Israeli atrocities and the array of forces behind some of the worst atrocities we have witnessed in recent history. No dissenting voices or rallies could capture the extent of genocide in Gaza and the barbarity to which Palestinians have been subjected. The irony of this reality is that it all happened out in the open, in front of all those who chose to open their eyes and see the brutalization of an entire people. Although the IDF has assassinated hundreds of journalists and kept others out of Gaza, the images of the unfolding genocide have been widely publicized on social media, including videos shared by Israeli soldiers.

The violence in Gaza has deeply scarred American and European liberal democracies. The political discourse of "Palestinian exceptionalism" has transformed American university campuses into battlefields for the defense of freedom of expression and the right to condemn Israeli atrocities. These campuses have played host to a revival of McCarthyist tactics. Princeton, my own employer at the time, was no exception. Rooting out antisemitism became a shibboleth around which many who otherwise rub shoulders with white supremacists mobilized an all-out attack on those who dared to raise their voices in defense of Palestinians, conveniently ignoring that a substantial portion of the protestors were Jewish.

Since this genocide began, I felt a sense of paralysis in writing about it. To me, the practice of writing always had something to do with the desire to explain a reality that otherwise remained hidden, to show that what we see is not necessarily what is happening below the surface. I am accustomed in my writing to address layers of contingencies, plots, actors, and institutions that interact with one another to shape a particular event. My ambivalence toward writing about Gaza came from the realization that the perpetrators of these savage acts saw no reason to hide their actions and the intentions behind them. Indeed, they wanted those acts *to be seen* by hundreds of millions of witnesses. That was deliberate. They wanted to boast that they possess such powers that afford them the ability, the right, to carry out a genocide with impunity.

As I reflected on the plight of Palestinians, the Israeli aggression with its American support, the perpetual demonization of Iran, repression on university campuses, and all the other trajectories that constitute the current moment, I saw the new events raise the same old questions of justice and accountability. There is, however, a difference in the way these events are enacted and the way most people see them. We have reached a point when nothing seems to shock us. All kinds of disasters, hurricanes, fires, floods, droughts, mass migrations, and even genocidal wars have become normalized events of our time. In so many ways, even the pretense of accountability no longer exists.

In 2016, when then-candidate Trump was running for his first presidency, he declared, "I could stand in the middle of Fifth Avenue and shoot somebody, and I wouldn't lose any voters, OK?" That was the moment Trump signaled that he would usher the US into a new era of brazen disregard for formal rules of governance and a flagrant contempt for accountability. I mean new in the sense that it was declared in the open and not only in secret boardrooms of corporations or government offices. Trump transformed the language of brutality, rape, racism, xenophobia, homophobia, and misogyny into an open element of normative political discourse and he continues to do so as the 47th President of the US.

States and non-state actors commit indefensible atrocities time and again. The long twentieth century was the bloodiest century in human history. These atrocities often happen as justification for a greater cause, that indeed has been the mantra of the post-Enlightenment ideology. As Herbert Marcuse noted, "We know that destruction is the price of progress as death is the price of life, that renunciation and toil are the prerequisites for gratification and joy, that business must go on, and that the alternatives are Utopian."[5] From colonial encounters of the eighteenth and nineteenth centuries to Trump's ambition to colonize Greenland, the logic of empire and capitalism has remained the same: the conquered needs to pay the price of progress, or in order to liberate you, we need to subjugate you. The famous Muslim critic of British colonialism in India, Seyyed Jamal al-Afghani, said it aptly in 1884 that "[the British] drew their sword to cut the throats of the Muslims, while weeping for them and crying: We kill you only out of compassion and pity for you and seeking to improve you and make your life comfortable."[6]

The genocide in Gaza has removed that kind of paradoxical pretense: war as a means of achieving peace, killing to save lives, subjugating

---

5 Herbert Marcuse, *One Dimensional Man*, Boston: Beacon, 1964. See chapter six: "From Negative to Positive Thinking: Technological Rationality and the Logic of Domination."

6 Al-Afghani, "Materialists in India," in Nikki Keddie, *An Islamic Response to Imperialism*, Berkeley & Los Angeles: University of California Press, 1968, p. 179.

to liberate. Murder, hatred, abuse, exclusion, discrimination, and silencing are all now done audaciously with impunity. All that is out in the open to be seen. This is the challenge of writing today. But this collection of essays is a reminder that the foundations of what we are now witnessing were laid decades ago. Many of those in American polity and in the corporate world who are scandalized by the brazenness of Trumpian political doctrine have been responsible for paving the road for the emergence of this authoritarianism. They are people who do not recognize their own role and certainly have never been called to account for their own actions.

This collection of essays documents the history behind the catastrophes we are witnessing today. In every turn, every moment, decisions were made by political actors that perpetuated states of war, injustice, and oppression. It is an attempt to compose a history of the present, a reminder of how a political ethos of indiscriminate brutality and a naked promotion of social injustice have become routinized and palatable as it unfolds in front of our eyes. It shows how the backstage curtain has fallen so we can all witness the loathsome realities of the contemporary political theater.

By the time this book is published, we might be living in a fundamentally different world. It is possible that Iran and the US could reach an agreement to contain Iran's nuclear technology in exchange for lifting the crippling sanctions the US has imposed against the Iranian people for decades. It is also possible that we could be in the middle of an all-out war between the two countries, a war that, without a shred of doubt, would engulf the entire region. These are the risks and futilities of writing in these uncertain days. What we write might melt into the air before it is even read. But the roots and conditions of possibility remain.

Collecting these essays in this volume is an exercise in exposing what the twenty-first-century order has brought—from the War on Terror to today's genocide in Gaza and the continuing dismantling of American liberal democracy. I hope to document and unmask the impunity with which this politics of hate and genocide unfold today. To show that despite their claims that these atrocities are committed for the salvation of all, will only lead to the annihilation of others. That is a step toward realizing the ethos that the great Italian Marxist, Antonio Gramsci, articulated as the "pessimism of the intellect, optimism of the will." The powerful will stay mighty so long as the legitimacy of their acts remains unquestioned and their authority uncontested.

SECTION I

IRAN
CENTERS OF POWER

The Islamic Republic's political system is an amalgam of theocratic rule, authoritarian institutions, electoral politics, and a resilient civil society. For more than four decades, factional politics, with competing ideological and strategic interests, and distinct sources of power and authority, have created a ruling class that is far from a monolithic political entity. Pundits and Western mass media often dismiss electoral processes and factional politics in Iran as an irrelevant and inconsequential political theater without any clout in the general tenor of the Islamic Republic. In these essays, I analyze the intricate power dynamics within the ruling class and demonstrate the importance of electoral politics in Iran, emphasizing why they merit serious consideration. Although the number of those who vote in elections has been declining, the ruling polity continues to consider public participation in electoral process to be a primary source of the legitimacy of the state. The conflict between the republicanism of the political order and its Islamic mandate remains as one of the constitutive tensions of the postrevolutionary regime in Iran.

1
What's the Matter with Iran?

July 2005

Thomas Frank opened his *What's the Matter with Kansas?* with a piercing sentence: "America is always in a state of quasi-civil war: on the one side are the unpretentious millions of authentic Americans; on the other stand the bookish, all-powerful liberals who run the country but are contemptuous of the tastes and beliefs of the people who inhabit it."[7] Frank recounted how the religious Right farmed a mass movement of social discontent that came to political fruition with the Reagan presidency. This movement generated an unlikely passionate alliance between growing numbers of the poor and the working class, Americans of the heartland, and the white middle class of suburbia. With Frank's account, it should no longer surprise us to see jobless laborers voting against their own

7 Thomas Frank, *What's the Matter with Kansas: How Conservatives Won the Heart of America,* New York: Metropolitan Books, 2005.

well-being for conservative politicians who advocate cutting unemployment benefits. Once a political force becomes hegemonic, it gains the power to lead its constituency towards any direction, albeit against their own immediate or long-term interests.

What does Kansas have to do with the Iranian presidential election? On June 24, 2005, Iranians chose Mahmoud Ahmadinejad by a large margin in a run-off election over Hashemi Rafsanjani as their president. Not only did this election stun the Iranian reformist camp, it also astonished the small coalition that sponsored Ahmadinejad's campaign. Since the first-term election of President Khatami in 1997, pundits and students of Iranian affairs took for granted that Iranian society was steadily retreating from its earlier Islamic Jacobin revolutionary politics. At the heart of this reform movement, it was believed, lay the easing of social restrictions on gender segregation, and a host of liberal rights such as freedom of expression, movement, and association. Although this reformist agenda remained far from realization, during his two-terms, Khatami encouraged the expansion of the institutions of civil society and championed the transformation of Iranian political discourse towards democratic pluralism. He succeeded to transform the political discourse but failed to turn his project into a hegemonic force in society.

Prior to last week's election, the coalition that brought Khatami to power, known as the Second of Khordad (May 23) Movement, concluded that Khatami lost much of his popular support due to his inability to push social reforms further and stand firm against the Supreme Leader's obstructionism and an antagonistic Judiciary. The idea of social reform became so entrenched in the Iranian political landscape that every qualified presidential candidate spoke in its terms. Even Mohsen Reza'i, the former head of the Revolutionary Guards, and Baqer Qalibaf, Tehran's former Police Chief, wrapped themselves in the cloak of the reformist agenda. Tehran's Police Chief even went as far as sending his advisers to seek guidance from Tony Blair's campaign managers on how to target the affluent middle classes of Tehran and repackage himself as a pro-reform candidate. All the presidential candidates, with the exception of the winner, agreed that the one who could successfully situate himself as the voice of social reform (that is, advocating rapprochement with the US, lessening the restrictions on women's mobility and claiming their legal rights, and recognizing "joy," i.e. dating, entertainment, coed public presence, as a basic right of youth) would win the election. In the morning after, we know that they were wrong.

Democracy, Iranian Style

Most of the American mass media followed the lead of the Bush administration in characterizing the election in Iran as an inconsequential "sham." For example, in an editorial on June 21, 2005, the *New York Times* called the election "a race for the mostly meaningless position of the president of Iran." The *Times'* editorial was written after the first round of the election which drew over 63 percent of eligible voters to the polls. Only if the editors had read the work of their own reporters in Tehran, would they have recognized the enthusiasm that many Iranians demonstrated on the streets of the big cities in the days and nights prior to the election. It is hard to imagine that kind of fervor for a "meaningless" position.

A chorus of Iranian expatriates also called for a boycott of the election. They argued that participating in an election marred by the Guardian Council's rejection of hundreds of candidates based on politically motivated qualification procedures, would legitimize the existing system. In order to justify their position, proponents of the boycott minimized the differences between the platforms of the opposing candidates and characterized them as variations on the same theme of Islamic totalitarianism. It is hard to imagine how they will reconcile the high turnout of the populace with their criterion for the legitimacy of the regime.

For many Iranian expatriates, Monarchists as well as the old-Left and new-Left cum liberal secularists, the problem of legitimacy does not rest on public participation. Their opposition to the Islamic regime is more ideological than procedural and political. For many expatriates, the problem of the legitimacy of this regime goes back to the 1979 revolution when one group was dethroned and the other lost the struggle over postrevolutionary state power. Although these groups ought to get a hearing in the court of history, they need to transcend their ideological commitments and engage with Iranian realpolitik. With a political strategy that demands regime change as its prerequisite, Iranian exilic communities risk joining their historical counterparts, the White Russians of Paris and the Cubans of Florida.

Democracy is an ongoing project that, as Chantal Mouffe once wrote, "always entails drawing a frontier between 'us' and 'them,' those who belong to the 'demos' and those who are outside of it."[8]

8 Chantal Mouffe, *The Democratic Paradox,* London, New York: Verso, 2000, p. 4.

The reformists stepped into the race when the Leader overruled the Guardian Council's disqualification of their main candidate, Mostafa Mo'in. By expanding his coalition to include banned liberal parties and personalities, Mo'in hoped that his campaign would attract the politically disgruntled and those who otherwise had decided to boycott the election. He ran on a platform of expansion of social reform, respect for human rights, civil liberties, unconditional release of all political prisoners (not in the thousands, but by all accounts in double digits), and a series of partly neo-liberal economic reforms for the sake of hopping on the train of globalization. On the day of the election, the Mo'in camp spoke of the possibility of capturing more than 50 percent of the vote, thereby winning the office without dragging the electorate into a run-off. With less than 14 percent of the vote, Mo'in came in fifth place and was eliminated.

The other oddball of the race was Mehdi Karrubi, a soft-spoken, unassuming cleric who was the Speaker of the reformist-dominated Sixth Parliament. No major political or religious institution openly endorsed his candidacy. Only Abdolkarim Soroush, an influential philosopher and lay theologian, lent his support to him by speculating that "since [Karrubi] has no enemies and no friends, he will be situated fittingly to negotiate with all factions productively." It turned out that Karrubi found many friends among the electorate and came in a close and contested third. He lost his chance to compete in the run-off by a few hundred thousand votes. Karrubi became the victim of the irregularities of the first round: voter intimidation and the massive mobilization of the Basiji Militia on behalf of conservative candidates. He should have pursued his allegations and pushed his way to the second round.

The most well-known candidate, Hashemi Rafsanjani, declared his intention to run after assurances from other factions that they would not engage in a smear campaign for alleged corruption and nepotism during his previous tenure as the president. Rafsanjani, as his campaign managers reinvented him, revitalized large groups of youth, men and women, and mobilized them through what they called "club Hashemi." The "club" organized dance parties and parades with banners and face paint reminiscent of British soccer fans. Women appeared without hijab on the streets under the auspices of Rafsanjani's campaign. Rafsanjani blurred the boundaries between northern Tehran and Westwood, as the appearance of his supporters became indistinguishable from the fashion-struck Iranians of Los Angeles. Women's makeup and face paint could not cover his past wrongs, and he lost his bid in the run-off with a humiliating 35 percent of the vote.

Why was everybody so wrong? Mohammad Quchani, a young and brilliant editor of the Tehran daily *Sharq*, noted that the recent election was the "defeat of reformism by democracy." Both Khatami and Ahmadinejad were swept into power by a wave of mass support that had been invisible prior to the day of the election. For Khatami in 1997, a silent discontent was brewing among the youth and women, who were then ready to step into the theater of electoral politics. And in 2005, another silence among the disinherited burst into demands to end corruption and manifested the good old conflict between the rich and the poor. Why has it been difficult to detect the emergence of these movements? To borrow again from Quchani, "politics in Iran have generally been a-social, political struggles often do not correspond to fundamental social rifts." The Iranian elite, no matter of which political persuasion, often miscalculates and misinterprets the constituents they allegedly represent. This is why Iranian politics oscillates too often between elitist political conflicts and massive populist outbursts.

What Lessons Do We Learn?

When it comes to elections, conspiracy theories abound. People tend to dismiss their own power and imagine their lives as controlled by an impervious political elite which installs favored candidates into contested elected positions. Electoral politics is universally vulnerable to apathy and disenfranchisement. Iranians are newcomers to this game and not yet affected completely by a chronic apathy. A great majority of the Iranian electorate genuinely believes that the system rewards their democratic participation. Everyone grappling with the results of this election must appreciate that the most significant lesson of this election was the act of participation. The more people believe in their own agency, the easier it is to engage them in social change and political reform. The further removed they are from political engagement, the stronger looms the opportunities for totalitarianism.

The result of this election is perhaps most astonishing to those who boycotted it, albeit it won't register in their minds as such. With a large turnout of the electorate (though they might dispute that, too), not only did their strategy fail but also the winner was a candidate who stood for everything they despise, from the aesthetics of his appearance to his rhetoric of Islamic social justice. The boycott camp is left with two options: first, question the validity of the tally and insist that the great majority of the people boycotted the election; second, question the maturity of the voters, and condemn the masses for their backwardness.

The reformists had the highest stakes in this election. For the first time since the 1979 revolution, many of the key figures of this camp have lost their footing inside the state apparatus. They should turn this unwanted blessing into a platform for mass mobilization and the expansion of their constituency. While the boycott camp fails to see the significance of political negotiation and the continuing possibility of top-down reform under the existing regime, the reformists neglect the importance of bottom-up pressure and the institutionalization of their agenda. They held the highest office but failed to become hegemonic. This failure created an atmosphere of mistrust against the Khatami administration reflected in the common complaint, why didn't he deliver on any of his promises? The reformist camp paid dearly for this mistaken identification of the President as the vanguard for social change. Rather than generating it, the President's proper responsibility was to create the political opportunity for social change. Social change ought to happen bottom-up, through institutionalized movements of rights and justice, but it needs to be recognized top-down.

In the absence of a top-down recognition, bottom-up social change leads to explosive revolutions. Conversely, without bottom-up institutionalization, top-down social changes lead to the alienation of the leaders and the disenfranchisement of the masses. Not only did the elitism of the reformists discredit Khatami, it also blinded them to the growing discontent that was quietly consuming their constituents.

The reformists had their greatest impact on the political discourse of the election. But unfortunately, the same impact brought the political fortunes of everyone who followed it to an abrupt end. From Tehran's police chief to the former head of the revolutionary guards and from the tsar of cultural repression to the Caesar of corruption, they all packaged themselves as the right candidate for reform. This reform, however, was not the kind of reform that could buy any of these contenders the presidency. What the reformists and their cheap duplicates learned was that the majority of the people did not share their conception of what reform in Iran means.

Under Khatami, reform became synonymous domestically with a movement for individual rights and civil liberties with a strong emphasis on its gendered dimension. Globally, it came to be understood as better relations with the Western world, particularly the US, and with their global financial institutions, the World Bank and the IMF. Without anybody looking, signing on to the onerous neo-liberal structural adjustments defined the political economy of reform in Iran. Somehow, somewhere in the middle of the road, instead of offering better negotiation power to resist the undemocratic and unjust conditions of the World Bank, individual rights and civil liberties movements became an instrument for making the country more attractive to IMF suitors.

The Iranian government is a colossal welfare state. It offers extensive subsidies for basic means of subsistence, from wheat to gas, public transportation to retirement benefits. Unless one has been reading too many of Tom Friedman's columns, no one should have any doubts that "joining the rest of the world," under the existing terms of the main global financial institutions, would have devastating consequences for the majority of the Iranian poor. The idea of encouraging investment and privatization of non-essential industries does not inherently undermine social justice. But the Iranian reformists should learn that liberty is the first victim of economic disparity, and social injustice is the inevitable consequence of repression.

The dogmatist ideologues of the revolution, the Guardian Council, the Supreme Leader, and now the president-elect, on one hand, and their ideological neoconservative counterparts in the White House, on the other, have the biggest lesson to learn. Although Mr. Ahmadinejad won the presidency, he must recognize that the undemocratic and unconstitutional arbitrary supervision of the Guardian Council undermines the legitimacy of his office. The recent election was indeed an indication that the ideological factions of the regime still enjoy popular support, and they still pose a viable political alternative in an electoral process. By electing Ahmadinejad, the electorate showed that they rather live in a society in which redistribution rather than accumulation of wealth defines the greatest Islamic virtue. The president-elect and his allies need to know that the commodities of the Western culture industry do not mesmerize all Iranians, and indeed many respect and value their religious and cultural particularities. The result of this election shows that even with an open and democratic election, this faction will not disappear from the Iranian political landscape. The freer the electoral process in Iran, the stronger the legitimacy of its institutions.

The president-elect also must avoid making the reformists' mistake and believe he captured the presidency in spite of other political currents in the country. Who wins in an election is partly made possible by those who run against him. Together, they legitimize the system.

The key to the success of this new president is the expansion of his constituency, speaking to the needs and demands of those who did not vote for him. That might prove to be an untenable position, but the mere fact of the recognition of the integrity and legitimacy of competing factions will make the Ahmadinejad administration domestically and globally more effective.

The American neoconservatives are slow learners. If reality does not match their perceptions, too bad, they declare, for reality. They should concede that the Islamic Republic bears no resemblance to Saddam Hussein's Iraq. The more they insist on regime change in Iran, the further they move away from an attainable solution to the conflict between the two countries. President Bush and Dr. Rice ought to listen more carefully to those who know Iranian politics rather than to their usual one-size-fits-all ideologues at the American Enterprise Institute and the Pentagon's Defense Policy Board. They should not simply ignore the 28 million Iranians who cast their ballots for a president and replay the broken record of "axis of evil" and regime change. Democracy is not good only in cases where its outcome is consistent with American interests. If, despite the unprecedented global unpopularity of President Bush, the rest of the world respects American citizens' choice for president, it should not be difficult for the Bush administration to return the favor and engage the Iranian president as a legitimate counterpart.

Whither Iran?

This election created conflicting emotions for many Iranians. Mr. Ahmadi-Nejad is the president of those who voted for him as well as those who did not. Many Iranians do not share his vision for the country, and they fear that he might take the country back to a time when violence was an integrated part of their everyday life. They fear that the new president might commit massive purges and persecutions. They fear that he will not be able to deliver his promises of prosperity and fairness to the Iranian poor. They hope that he will not pursue an antagonistic policy against the Western powers, and that he will realize that a strong international position requires just and respectful domestic governance.

The hope is that the president-elect is true to his words when he declared, "today we have only two-degree of the possible 360-degree of freedom." Iranians will see him next time at the ballot box to assess his degrees of freedom and the extent of prosperity he has mustered for his constituency at the end of his term.

2
The Donkey and the Date

December 2006

On December 15, Iranians will cast their ballots for municipal elections. Reformist candidates across the country, particularly in Tehran, have a credible opportunity to win, if their constituents emerge from their hibernation and actively participate in these elections. The government has hindered the domestic media's attempt to generate a celebratory environment for the electorate to exercise their constitutional right. Iranian media around the world need to realize that a dampened-down election will only perpetuate the status quo and will reinforce a growing messianic belief that Iranians need to be rescued.

The famous American sociologist Harold Garfinkel observed that people become conscious of the order of things around them only when that order is disrupted. The taken-for-granted thus exists invisibly until its existence is breached.

Since his election in 2005, Mahmoud Ahmadinejad's administration has ceaselessly restricted civil liberties and political rights. Numerous opposition parties and personalities rightfully publicize these violations and emphasize the importance of legal and political protection of civil liberties as the foundation for any future transformation of the Iranian society. But many of these same groups have been relentlessly denying the existence of these liberties in the Islamic Republic in the first place. If the Ahmadinejad administration has banned the publication and the reprint of numerous books, if they have reinstituted secret prisons, if they refuse permits for demonstrations, if they close newspapers indefinitely without a court order, if government officials have refused to be accountable for their actions to the Majlis, if all of these changes are indeed happening don't they suggest that there had been a different political configuration in place before they were effected? Could it be that the Khatami presidency accomplished things that are now being disrupted? We become more aware of the achievements of Khatami when we witness their disappearance.

In his first interview after leaving office, in response to a reporter who asked about his best moment as president, Khatami referred to his address at Tehran University on the occasion of Student Day in 2004. During his speech, enraged students interrupted and denounced him for yielding to the conservative judiciary in pursuing his project of strengthening the institutions of civil society. He listened quietly with open displeasure and left after hearing out his opponents. He told the reporters, that was his finest moment in office! For the first time in the country's history a leader faced shouting critics in an open forum and not a single person was arrested afterwards. Before Khatami, this would have been unimaginable in Iran and is perhaps no longer possible even in the US today.

There is an expression in Farsi that describes people who want contradictory things: those who want both the donkey and the date. These are people who are never mistaken and see all situations in the context of their own interests. Iranians and their Euro-American supporters, those who advocate boycotting every election in the Islamic Republic, cannot have it both ways. They cannot argue that the office of the president (and all other elected offices) is politically impotent, while also lamenting the repressive nature of the Ahmadinejad presidency and how he is taking the country back to its early postrevolutionary period. This poses a dilemma for these universal boycotters. If elected officers make a difference, for worse or better, then why shouldn't citizens vote? There are many different positions on this question ranging from single-minded abolitionists, whose agenda is regime change in Iran, with or without the help of their neocon brethren, to those who recognize the differences between different factions, but argue that participating in elections legitimizes authoritarian institutions such as the Guardian Council. Although the reasons for boycotting elections may differ, the result is the same: low voter participation has devastating consequences for reform candidates.

The boycotters, the civilized ones, believe that the only path to change in Iran is through a general referendum on the constitution of the Islamic Republic. When asked how this might be possible, regime-change advocates outline a program of civil disobedience which, if massive, would coerce the ruling coterie to relinquish its power and accept the terms and results of the referendum.

Unfortunately, *tark-e 'adat mujeb-e maraz-ast,* old habits die hard. One of the principal shortcomings in Iranian political culture is the lack of enduring, persistent, and patient mobilization from below. The old political left (Islamic or secular) subscribed to a Jacobin form of politics, passionately believing that social change could only be realized top-down by decapitating the state. While many boycotters don't endorse violence, they still hold out hope for the single blow, the referendum, that would terminate the Islamic regime. Piecemeal transformation does not exist in the political lexicon of the Iranian left (or right). Politics Iranian style borrows heavily from Bazaari culture: Herculean in the wholesale, horrendous in the retail.

As for me, I oppose any party that hopes to claim victory in a not-so-likely-referendum in a not-so-possible-future. I know this because contrary to those who believe that the chief problem in Iranian politics is that the wrong people are in power (that might as well be true), the real problem is structural: power corrupts its wielders. There is only one way that this predicament can change: expanding the formal and informal institutions in which citizens participate actively and regularly. Politics does not begin and end with voting. Nor is civic participation monumental or spectacular. Citizens practice their economic, political, and social responsibilities in countless ways: in their workplaces, professional associations, neighborhoods, and schools. Along with the criticism one might make of President Khatami's weakness, naivete, or passivity, those citizens of the Islamic Republic who themselves failed to institutionalize political reforms in myriad municipal and professional organizations should also be held culpable for failing to strengthen civil society.

Iranians have another chance on December 15 to practice their rights and responsibilities in municipal and city council elections around the country. In order to defeat reformist candidates who have somehow survived the disqualification procedures and still appear on the ballot, the Judiciary, the ministries of Culture and Islamic Guidance, Information, and Domestic Affairs, the state-controlled radio and television, and the conservative newspapers have all been mobilized to ensure low participation of the electorate. The judiciary spokesperson has threatened the newspapers that run front-page news of the election with closure and censure.

Iranian expatriates with access to mass media should counter this strategy by turning the municipal elections into a welcome political event. It is imperative for Iranians at home and abroad to participate in these elections. The more engaged people remain with these processes, the harder it becomes for any institution in society to trample on their wishes. An empowered reformist city council in Tehran, or any other municipality in the country, could achieve modest, but genuine changes in the way the city is managed and the way its residents live. While most Iranian expatriates remain impervious towards modest changes in daily life, we should realize that what seems negligible to us often has remarkable consequences for our fellow citizens inside the country. Incremental changes are only irrelevant to those whose lives are untouched by those changes.

3
Iran's 2006 Elections

December 2006

On December 15, more than 60 percent of Iranians cast ballots in municipal elections. With the mounting pressure of reformist coalitions, a remarkable number of their candidates survived the draconian vetting processes of the clerical establishment and turned this election into a popular vote of confidence in Ahmadinejad's administration. Whether they succeed in winning the majority seats in city and town councils in Tehran and other parts of the country is not known yet. But the mere act of the electorate's massive participation once more exhibited the resilience of democratic institutions under the Islamic Republic in spite of abundant social, legal, and political impediments. Had this election occurred in an allied country of the US, it would have been celebrated as the highest achievement of American foreign policy. But the Bush administration and the mainstream media disregard elections held under an alleged "totalitarian" state as a non-event.

There is an expression in Persian that if a wall's first brick is laid unevenly, it will be skewed no matter how high it is erected. President Bush won his first term by corrupting the votes in Florida and later by exploiting the judicial system in the US. This set a devastating precedent for an administration that considers itself to be above the law and believes it can wield its power indiscriminately around the world. It is indeed one of the most appalling ironies that a President who assumed office fraudulently calls himself and his entourage of neoconservative hawks the messengers of democracy in the world. He might be right in believing that his mission of spreading democracy in the world defines his presidency. But the problem is that for this administration, like many others before it, democracy means turning a nation into an American ally. According to Bush, the world is divided into three camps: undemocratic, countries impervious to American interests; democratic, countries yielding to American interests; and those in between. There is nothing novel about this strategic narcissism. American foreign policy during the Cold War was informed by the tunnel vision of "American interests" which compelled one administration after another to raise the heat of the Cold War through successive proxy wars and coup d'états, think Iran 1953, Guatemala 1954, Indonesia 1967, Vietnam 1965-73, Chile 1973, Afghanistan, Angola, Nicaragua 1980s, and the list goes on.

The US learned the wrong lessons in the Cold War. A nation's right to self-determination, even at the expense of American interests, must be respected. The US is not the Supreme Leader of the world with power to override the outcome of elections in other countries. When the Palestinians cast their ballots in favor of Hamas, or the Venezuelans elect Chavez as their president, it is morally wrong and politically bankrupt to punish them with economic sanctions or conspire to overthrow their legitimate government because the White House believes that the people have elected the "wrong party." The Cold War is over, but the worldview that gave rise to it thrives.

President Bush's advisors would greatly benefit from reading Iranians' numerous letters to the BBC's Persian service and interviews with Iranian daily newspapers about why they vote or alternatively why they boycott the elections. The majority who vote do so consciously to underline their preference for a homegrown democracy with all its faults over an imported American brand. One constituent wrote, "I voted to prove that our true desire is to transform this system, and to show that we don't need American democracy." Another letter from Shahin Shar noted, "There is no room to breathe freely, Iran's international credibility and respect is diminishing, and we hope that we are not on a path to war, I voted to change this direction." "I want to know," another interviewee from Tehran asked rhetorically, "in which other country in the world do they have carnivals on the streets and the artists and celebrities go to neighborhoods to encourage people to participate?"

Another woman from Golestan described her vote as a "declaration against right-wing populism and US warmongering." Another voter from Mashad aptly observed, "Iranians always believe that the neighbor's grass is greener [. . .] I am 62 years old, and I vote proudly in all elections. I exercise this right and feel sorry for those who fall short of their responsibilities and wait for some invisible hand to come and rescue them. I know that they are inexperienced and do not have any idea about other parts of the world. I ask them to look at the Arab countries, all of those with good relations with the US and tell me that they are more democratic than we are." A young voter from Shiraz called the election a "velvet revolution" that will strengthen "local decision-making and non-governmental organizations."

Since President Bush has announced that he has been on a listening tour, maybe he ought to extend the length of this most unusual campaign and listen to the words and actions of the people he wants to rescue in Iran.

4
The Iranian Revolution Turns Forty: Dare to Know, Have the Courage to Act!

February 2019

Legend has it that in 1972, when the Chinese Premier Zhou Enlai was asked about the impact of the French Revolution, his response was that "it's too soon to say." Although the accuracy of the story has been questioned, I believe that legendary response remains historically apposite. What revolutions do, their failure or success, their lasting impact, their tangible and intangible achievements are often expressed in contradictory terms and difficult to ascertain. The Iranian revolution of 1979 is not an exception. Iranians mark the fortieth anniversary of their revolution at a moment that cries of regret are commonly heard all over the country, in rural areas as well as in urban centers. These voices are openly heard on the streets of big cities and small towns, among the downtrodden and affluent classes alike. The discontent is also echoed and encouraged by a host of exilic media, American and European Persian TV and radio networks, mourning the revolution and romanticizing the *ancien régime*. These broadcasts highlight ongoing corruption, repression, cultural and social alienation, gender and ethnic discrimination, economic hardship, and regional destabilization. And of course, every year on the anniversary of the revolution the question is asked for how much longer the regime will last, a question that is as old as the revolution itself.

Those grievances are legitimate, particularly the problem of corruption and the deepening of social inequality. This is not a secret. It is discussed in every single session of the Iranian Parliament and widely written about in newspapers and op-ed pieces inside Iran. Almost invariably in these discussions, intellectuals, pundits, government officials, and members of the parliament still invoke the authority of revolutionary discourse to warn about the growing cleavage between the promises of the revolution and the realities of everyday life in the country. Long are gone the days that Ayatollah Beheshti, the once powerful Vice Chair of the Constitutional Assembly and the influential Head of the Judiciary until his assassination in 1981, set the goal of the distribution of wealth in society to a one-to-three ratio between the lowest and the highest income. That egalitarian mantra lives but only as a shibboleth with no correspondence with the facts of life.

All that is true. But should one question the wisdom of revolutionary transformation that ended the autocratic rule of the Shah, repositioned Iran as a regional power, and turned Iran into a vibrant, rights-conscious, participatory, and engaged society? The revolutionary will that once toppled the fifth largest military in the world with bare hands and marching feet also brought a historical awakening to Iran that shapes the collective consciousness of the nation to this day. That consciousness continues to manifest itself in different forms of dissent and civic engagement.

The revolution in Iran happened at the time when the very idea of revolution had become suspect in intellectual circles in the West. The disillusionment of the European Left with both the Soviet and the Chinese experiments, and their own failure to mount a revolutionary campaign after 1968, made the ideas of utopia and revolution increasingly synonymous with totalitarianism and the reign of terror. At the time, the disenchanted European Left joined the chorus of liberals calling terror an inherent feature of revolution and radical transformation of society a foreboding utopia.

The Iranian revolution shared its spirit with postcolonial Afro-Asian and Caribbean resistance movements that changed the axis of politics in the world from the East-West antagonism to the South-North struggles. It was a revolution that, like many others around the globe, sought to shore up the nation's right of self-determination and by doing so rearrange the global political and economic hierarchies that sustained an imperialist world order. The Iranian revolution was the embodiment of a spirit that enchanted the world of the downtrodden from Manley's Jamaica to Sukarno's Jakarta, from Cape Town to Cairo, from Managua to Manila. Iranians were dreaming that they could build a just world. In Iran, the spirit engulfed the entire nation and brought with it an enduring sense of empowerment that now enters its fortieth anniversary. The courage displayed during the revolutionary movement, the fearlessness that propelled the revolution forward, the dignity with which the masses asserted themselves, and the determination manifested in history-making marches and strikes created a new nation that continues to exercise its audacity, creativity, and confidence.

Forty years ago, imperialism, colonialism, capitalism, and individualism were conditions that a great majority of people around the world demanded to overcome. Justice, equality, equity, and participatory governance were not markers of intellectual distance between visionaries and the disinherited masses. Today, that revolutionary vernacular sounds passé and obsolete. A whole industry of anti-revolution propaganda, informed by a global network of neoliberal top-down, controlled, piecemeal modernization, dominates the way many think about the Iranian revolution and other radical political experiments in the global South. Now, a commonplace view renders revolution as an infantile disorder to reshape a world that has already reached the end of its history–what we have is what we get.

Forty years ago, Iranians embodied the German philosopher Walter Benjamin's definition of revolution and took a leap into the open sky of possibilities, a costly leap into a world of uncertainty. Forty years later, the Iranian exilic media, with their massive capital, and the same imperialist powers whose interests the revolution contained, manufacture nostalgia of prerevolution days of glory. Days when an autocratic monarch slowly but steadily carried his nation through the "gates of great civilization," as he used to proudly stress, toward a future that promised to revive the grandeur of the ancient past– only if his flock quietly and obediently followed his lead with eyes closed, heads down, and mouths shut.

Today, an invigorating civil society, massive engagement of women in public affairs, an ingenious cinema, exemplary artistic and intellectual productions and networks in Iran exist because of, and not despite, the revolution. The revolution has left a legacy of fundamental transformation of the way people see the world, relate to themselves and to others, understand rights and responsibilities, and hold those in power accountable for what they do and what they refuse to do. There is no question that the leap Iranians took forty years ago let them to a perilous road through the reign of terror, war, international political strain and debilitating sanctions. This anniversary belongs to those who believed and continue to believe that courage and dignity cannot be burdened by fear and obedience.

5

The Electoral Politics and Legitimation Crisis in Iran

June 2021

Last week, Iran's Guardian Council[9] disqualified an entire class of politically diverse candidates from running in the next month's presidential election. The Council certified only seven candidates, one of whom, Ayatollah Ibrahim Raisi, the current Head of the Judiciary, is unmistakably designated to be the next president of the Islamic Republic. The Council axed all the candidates who could even remotely jeopardize Raisi's chances, including the three-time speaker of the Parliament, former two-term president, Mahmoud Ahmadinejad, the current vice president, and many other influential politicians and political activists. The Council's intention to secure a victory for Raisi, was so evident that even the Ayatollah himself pleaded with the Council

9 For its role and responsibilities see: https://www.britannica.com/topic/Council-of-Guardians

to "make the election more competitive." The general feeling in the country is that the Council has appointed Raisi, whose original claim to fame was his membership in the infamous "death commission" in late 1980s that carried out the execution of thousands of political prisoners, as the president, rendering the election pointless.

Ever since Ayatollah Khomeini first spoke of his desire to establish an Islamic Republic in Iran, a critical mass of the high-ranking clerics, whether openly or discreetly, have expressed their displeasure with the concept of republicanism. They have remained suspicious of any attempt that recognizes the sovereignty of the people as the foundation of the legitimacy of state power. The following interview published in *Le Monde* on November 13, 1978, laying out his vision, gave rise to deep discontent among members of the clergy who considered themselves to be either the guardians of the constitutional monarchy or the advocates of its overthrow to be replaced by a theocratic religious state.

> *Le Monde*: Your Excellency wishes to establish an Islamic Republic in Iran. For the French people this is ambiguous, because a republic cannot have a religious foundation. Is your republic based on socialism? Constitutionalism? Would you hold elections? Is it democratic?
> *Ayatollah Khomeini*: Our republic has the same meaning as anywhere else. We call it 'Islamic Republic' because the conditions of its emergence are embedded in Islam, but the choice belongs to the people. The meaning of the republic is the same as any other republics in the world.[10]

10 Behrooz Ghamari-Tabrizi, *Islam and Dissent in Postrevolutionary Iran,* London, New York: Bloomsbury, 2008, p. 50.

Republicanism, as Khomeini elaborated in a number of future occasions, was about granting sovereignty to people and recognizing their right of self-determination. The idea that teachings of Islam and its divinely inspired politics guided the republic did not register to Ayatollah Khomeini and his followers as an inherent contradiction in a system in which the primary source of state legitimacy was considered to be electoral politics. For them, there existed no contradiction between Islamic teachings and popular will. They argued that a "true" Islamic practice cannot contradict the will of the people, if it does, then it is not Islamic. For more than forty years, the Islamic Republic has been grappling with this very singular predicament–how to reconcile the sovereignty of the people with Islamic foundations of governance.

Since 1979, every presidential election in Iran has drawn an average of 65-70 percent of the eligible voters to the polls, and generated an intense carnivalesque atmosphere in the entire country. People used to celebrate their candidates for weeks prior to the election day in rallies, marches, and dances in the streets. The whole country became colorful and festive. More than supporting one candidate over another, what people celebrated every four years was the right of self-determination. They desired their candidate to win, but more importantly, they wanted to reiterate the significance of the office of the president and one of the pillars of the postrevolutionary state.

The Guardian Council's mass disqualification of presidential candidates is the outcome of a forty-year-long project of gradual but systematic encroachment of the theocratic institutions of power in Iran against republicanism and the democratic impulse of the 1979 revolution. These kinds of disqualification are by no means new. But this round of intervention, both qualitatively and quantitatively, was exceptional. With the announcement of the Council's decision came a series of coordinated sermons and statements to redefine the very meaning of legitimacy and sovereignty. Friday imams and commentators close to the Council desperately tried to delink the question of legitimacy from public participation. "Low participation," said Mr. Kadkhodai, the Guardian Council's spokesperson, "has nothing to do with the legitimacy of the election."[11] Another member of the Assembly of Experts opined that "elections are means by which the people express their allegiance to the existing order."[12] Those who do not fulfill this obligation, that is participating in the election, asserted the influential Friday Prayer Imam of the holy city of Mashad and the father-in-law of Ayatollah Raisi, "could no longer be regarded as Muslims."[13]

Those inside the Iranian polity who had believed the internal transformation of the political order still feasible, would now face a seemingly unresolvable conundrum. For more than four decades, they endeavored to highlight the democratic potential of the republic by mobilizing around parliamentary and presidential elections. They offered a viable alternative to those who advocate regime change and toppling of the Islamic Republic as the only path toward democratization of the Iranian political system. The reformists are

11 https://www.radiofarda.com/a/ap-interview-iran-presidential-candidates-kadkhodaee-guardian-council/31261764.html

12 https://www.etemadonline.com/

13 https://www.asriran.com/

now shut out of electoral politics. They no longer see themselves as part of a state they had played a crucial role in building. By eliminating the reformist factions, the Guardian Council terminated the strategy that one of the key figures in reformist politics in Iran, Said Hajjarian, had formulated as *bargaining on the top, pressuring from below*. What is now left for the loyal opposition is pressure from below— the expansion and strengthening of the institutions of civil society. Whether such pressures will eventually lead to the kind of political transformations the reformists desire or that transformation could only occur through the overthrow of the Islamic Republic is yet to be seen.

Political transformation in Iran has always been intertwined with American policies in the region. What might not be known in the outside world is that there exists a vibrant civil society, publishers, women's groups, human rights organizations, public intellectual forums, mass and social media communities, growing labor organizations, environmentalists, etc. These groups became increasingly more vulnerable to the state security apparatus amid escalating external pressure and the imposition of draconian sanctions under Trump administration. Not only did the Trump-Pompeo doctrine of "maximum pressure" fail to sway Iran's regional and international positions by forcing the Islamic Republic to accommodate American and its allies' interests in the region, more importantly, maximum pressure also afforded justification to the state security apparatus to impose more repressive measures against civil society actors.[14] The

14 https://theconversation.com/iran-us-policy-of-maximum-pressure-has-failed-why-the-west-needs-to-re-engage-tehran-153011

maximum pressure led to a minimum gain in the US and the intensification of the security state in Iran.

The Trump administration's exit from the nuclear agreement wrecked political processes of rapprochement in Iran similar to George W. Bush's "Axis of Evil" State of the Union address in 2002. With their belligerent positions, Bush and Trump undercut Iranian reformists by discrediting their policies of appeasement and reconciliation. Bush called Iran an axis of evil as the Iranian government offered logistical and political support to topple the Taliban in Afghanistan. Trump pulled out of the nuclear agreement despite Iran's full compliance and the hope that the agreement could usher in a new chapter in Iran-US relations. In both cases, the results were catastrophic for the Iranian state politics—an open invitation to the hardliners to extend their political and popular base.

What is at stake today, the dominant factions in the state argue, is the territorial integrity of the country which is now threatened by hostile Western interventions and their domestic collaborators. Maximum pressure has produced a uniform, securitized, *state of exception* in Iran, the latest manifestation of which is the Guardian Council's attack on the very institution of the presidential elections. For all practical purposes, the Council has appointed the next president by barring others from competing in the race against Ayatollah Raisi. The hardliners in Iran incessantly warn the opposition that undermining the state authority will inevitably lead to the "Syrianization of Iran." The Guardian Council's decision Assadized the Iranian presidency—elections without an electorate.

Whether the June election will set the precedent for the future of electoral politics in Iran is yet to be determined. Much depends on Raisi, how he performs in the office, how successful his administration is in checking dissent and the demands of civil society, and finally, how the Biden administration will redefine the misguided US Middle East strategy and pay heed to the voices of change from inside Iran rather than fulfilling the demands of Iran's regional adversaries such as Israel and Saudi Arabia.

SECTION II

IRAN-US TURBULENT RELATIONS

Ever since the 1979 revolution that deposed the US-backed Shah, Iran has remained a major foreign policy challenge for the US. Although Iran remains determined to maintain its sovereign power and exercise regional influence, the Islamic Republic poses no direct security threat to the US. Yet even decades after the hostage crisis, Iran is regularly framed in such terms by American political actors and commentators. In these essays, I take on this paradox, addressing how successive administrations in the US have failed to grasp the scope of the Islamic Republic's strategic aims in the region, and the effects of this misreading. Throughout the past two decades, various agencies and actors who shape American foreign policy have manufactured crises, particularly in regard to Iran's nuclear enrichment program, to force Iran to submit to the demands of the US and its regional allies. The 2025 American-Israeli unprovoked war on Iran was the outcome of years of misrepresentation and demonization of the Islamic Republic.

6

Disturbing Opportunism: Change in Iran ought to flourish without external threats of violence and invasion

May 2003

Recently, two statements on the necessity and urgency of fundamental political change in Iran have been distributed via the internet. The first is authored by a group called The International Committee for A Transition to Democracy in Iran (CITDI, the acronym for its French title). More than 200 Iranian scholars, political pundits, and activists signed a second statement called "For the Unity of Iranian Republicans."[15]

15 https://iranian.com/Opinion/2003/May/Republic/index.html

CITDI's membership includes an impressive list of celebrated left-leaning intellectuals, scientists, and artists, such as Samir Amin, Noam Chomsky, Costa Gavras, Edward Said, Immanuel Wallerstein, Harold Pinter, etc.

The core agenda of both statements is a call for a general referendum in Iran with the intention of founding a "secular parliamentarian republic" based on respect for "the principles and values enunciated in the Universal Declaration of Human Rights," and its other ensuing democratic proclivities.

In its statement, CITDI asserts that the bottomless appetite of Washington hawks for expanding their control over the vast resources of the region has made the need for change in Iran an urgent necessity. They argue that "in order to avoid a further extension of the disastrous conflicts in the region," all democratic forces in the world ought to be mobilized and lend their support to their Iranian counterparts to bring about a "preemptive peace."

This objective is realizable "through bringing pressure to bear on the cleric rats in power in order to compel them to yield to the will of the people who demand a referendum for the establishment of a secular and democratic republic."

The Manifesto of Iranian Republicans also emphasizes the "dead-end of reform" in Iran. The Manifesto stresses that the Islamic Republic's continuing anti-democratic policies have undermined Iranian national interests in the world community, and it warns, in an implicit reference to Washington hawks, that these policies have now endangered the sovereignty of the nation and its territorial integrity.

I have no objection to the basic premise of these statements; the Iranian political infrastructure should undergo a fundamental transformation. Also, as colleagues, friends, and contributors to social thought and defenders of the just and the good, I have tremendous respect for many of the signatories of both statements.

However, what compels me to write these lines is the disturbing opportunism which lies in between the lines of their statements. Warning the Iranian regime to submit to the will of the Iranian people or be subjected to the wrath of Washington hawks is inadvertently playing the good cop to the threats of American administration bullies.

Although democratic reform in Iran is a legitimate demand, coupling it with the threat of a war of invasion strikes me as a Left opportunistically riding the wave of American imperialism. Such a position would neither bring about genuine change in Iran, nor would it contain American expansionist ambitions. Worse than stalled reform in Iran would be change induced by the peril of foreign invasion.

The "reform movement" in Iran was the result of the simultaneous expansion of the institutions of civil society and the emergence of a new polity from within the Islamic Republic, inspired by and with the support of a new Muslim intelligentsia. This movement is indeed far from a homogeneous effort for political and social change in Iran.

However, all participants of this movement share a desire to resolve the inherent contradictions in the sources of legitimacy of the state both in the Iranian constitution and in the realpolitik of the regime. The significance of this multifaceted movement, mostly known for its remarkable and unprecedented intellectual production, is in its transformative rather than abolitionist impulse. Let me clarify what I mean.

The Manifesto of Iranian Republicans starts with this passage: "After a century of struggle for transition from autocracy to democracy and from tradition to modernity, our people are at the thresholds of a new movement for the realization of their lasting aspirations."

Iranian intellectuals have primarily been influenced by the French tradition of Jacobinist social change which tends to thrive more on rupture and abolishment than continuity and transformation. Anything old is suspect and ought to be dismantled, thus the bifurcation of "tradition and modernity."

This dichotomous way of thinking conceives modernity and all its foundational principles (i.e., secularism, democracy, human rights, individualism, etc.) in contradistinction with tradition (i.e., superstition, religion, despotism, patriarchy, etc.). In the last one hundred years, Iranian intellectuals have been vacillating between the defending modernity as an imported commodity and cherishing tradition as a vehicle to fend off the invasion of the modern.

For the first time in Iranian history, the reform movement in Iran has transformed the dichotomy of "tradition versus modernity" into the tradition of modernity. Rather than conceptualizing tradition and modernity in mutually exclusive categories, for the new reform movement in Iran the modern emerges from the re-articulation of the traditional.

This movement needs to pave a long and arduous path. A sustainable change in Iran requires a bottom-up development of civil society, a meaningful intellectual engagement with the defenders and interpreters of Iranian traditions, and an organized effort for political and legal reform to ensure unrestricted expansion of the first two elements of change.

The expectation that President Khatami or the current reform-minded parliament will change the political apparatus of the Islamic Republic in any fundamental way is misleading and unproductive. It is only based on this mistaken expectation that the authors of the Manifesto of Iranian Republicans and many others inside Iran stress the dead-end of Iranian political reform. The reform movement was neither the brainchild of the President and his fellow 2nd of Khordad companions, nor will it reach its end with their demise.

It is the responsibility of Iranian intellectuals and other supporters of democratic movements in Iran to allow these movements to flourish on their own terms. Using the threats of American messianic hawks as a leverage to force a referendum or any fundamental change in Iran is detrimental to democratic processes not only in Iran, but also in the US and around the world.

I believe it is the responsibility of all those signatories of CITDI and the Manifesto to de-legitimize and expose the real intentions of the Bush administration and bring democratic processes back to the US The CITDI press communiqué warned the Islamic Republic that if they fail to act now, "it would be very difficult to avoid the outbreak of a civil war in Iran, whose consequences would be as devastating as incalculable." I find it offensive that in the face of flagrant American warmongering, members of CITDI put the responsibility of war or peace in the region squarely on the shoulders of the Iranian regime.

Change should and will happen in Iran, but this process ought to flourish without external threats of violence and invasion. Nobody should use the power of the American Empire to blackmail another country for social, political, and economic change, no matter how legitimate those changes might be.

Socially conscious intellectuals need to check the imperialist ambitions for US expansionism from within the US. Threats alluded to in the CITDI documents will not bring about lasting changes in Iran, their exploitation by the respected members of CITDI and Iranian Republicans can only be detrimental to the cause they are advocating.

The real threat to peace in the region and around the world is the Bush Administration. The threat of violence and war has never produced a lasting peace. The experience of the last two years (since President Bush's infamous axis of evil speech at the State of the Union address) shows that pointing American guns at the Iranian regime strengthens undemocratic tendencies in Iran and pushes the country defensively towards the erection of a national security apparatus.

In order to assist reform in Iran, the responsibility of every democratically inclined person is to deny the Iranian regime the opportunity to suspend civil and political liberties as a result of the American threat. Regime change starts at home, our home is here in America, let's get on with it.

7

Is the US on a Collision Course with Iran?

September 2004

On July 20, 2004, Senator Rick Santorum (R-PA) introduced the Iran Freedom and Support Act of 2004, a legislation promoting the transformation of the Islamic Republic of Iran to a democratic form of government. In justifying his co-sponsorship, with Senator John Cornyn (R-TX), of the Act, Senator Santorum lambasted the Iranian government for its "aggressive actions to support terrorist organizations," its "ballistic missile program," "violence against Americans in Iraq," "hiding information about its nuclear activities," and a host of other charges that make the Islamic Republic a threat to the national security of the US of America. "This legislation," Santorum concludes, "expresses the sense of the

Congress that it should be the policy of the US to support regime change in Iran."[16]

The reckless brandishing of regime change, which has become the cliché of neo-con politics, does not ease tensions over the Iranian nuclear technology. The policy of regime change negates constructive engagement; the two cannot coexist. A negotiated settlement with the Iranian government over its nuclear technology cannot emerge from undermining the sovereignty of the Islamic Republic. Without advocating a scenario of Armageddon, we need to recognize that the absence of détente in the political lexicon of the Bush Administration is spiraling the Middle East into an irreversible nuclear arms race.

At stake is the Iranian government's two nuclear plants, built largely by the Russian contractors. The government in Tehran insists that its nuclear program pursues a peaceful purpose, and as President Khatami reiterated recently, Iran has no interest in developing nuclear weapons. Of course, one cannot accept the assurances of an embattled president whose two terms in office were mired with internal conflicts. Khatami's office was powerless to challenge the Supreme Leader and the judiciary. The positions expressed by Iranian officials do not guarantee that Iran would utilize its nuclear technology solely for generating electricity and not for bomb-grade enriched uranium. With American forces knocking on its doors from all sides of its borders, a nuclear Pakistan in the southeast, and a nuclear Israel making daily threats of striking its enrichment facilities, it would be naïve to

16 https://www.iranwatch.org/library/government/united-states/congress/legislation-reports/s-2681-iran-freedom-and-support-act-2004

think that at least some factions in the Iranian government do not fancy nuclear weapons.

Iran is a signatory to the Non-Proliferation Treaty (NPT). The current crisis surfaced when Iran failed to report the construction of a new nuclear plant near the city of Natanz to the International Atomic Energy Agency (IAEA). To correct the breach of contract, the IAEA asked Iran to agree to an additional protocol that gave it unrestricted access to all Iranian nuclear facilities, as well as the right to unannounced spot inspection. The Iranian parliament approved the additional protocol and asked for assurances that in exchange for unrestricted access and spot inspection the "Big-Three" Europeans (UK, France, and Germany) would share nuclear technology with Iran.

While after months of inspection the IAEA found no evidence of a weapons program and stated that Iran is in no violation of the NPT, the US and EU remain unsatisfied with the level of transparency of the Iranian nuclear program. The Bush Administration asserts, a view echoed by Senator John Kerry, that the only solution for this standoff is that Iran must "prove they are not building weapons." Putting the negative burden of proof that they are not building weapons on Iranian shoulders should be familiar to us all. Like Saddam Hussein in the months preceding the war, the accused bears the burden of proving his innocence.

But regardless of the exchanges between the IAEA and the Iranian government, similar to its attitude toward the UN inspection team in Iraq, the Bush Administration appropriated the IAEA position as a smokescreen for its ambitions in the region. In its last meeting in Vienna, Director General Muhammad al-Baradei expressed satisfaction with the progress of IAEA work in Iran, while emphasizing that there remained much work to be done. He asked Iran to halt its enrichment activities voluntarily, since, as an NPT signatory, Iran enjoys the right to enrich uranium without breaching the treaty. After the Vienna meeting, John Bolton, the undersecretary of state for arms control and international security, boasted that Iran's conduct did not "bode well for the success of a negotiated approach to dealing with this issue." Mr. Bolton left nothing opaque about the meaning of a non-negotiated approach when he compared the situation in Iran with that of South Africa and Ukraine, both of which abandoned their military nuclear programs after the fall of the *ancien régime*. If the administration's point man for negotiating a settlement does not believe in negotiation and advocates the change of the regime with which he is supposed to engage, it is easy to see why the Islamic Republic remains skeptical of American intentions. Why should it negotiate with a state that openly advocates its overthrow?

The US position on the Iranian nuclear technology has also generated confusion in the media. We know that this Administration is not a reliable source of information. It regards intelligence as politics by other means. Recent articles in the New York Times and reports on NPR on the Iranian nuclear activities repeat the same kind of unconfirmed allegations that turned authoritative journalists into drumbeaters for war with Iraq. For example, the title of Steven Weisman's diplomatic memo in the *New York Times* read "Bush Aides Divided on Confronting Iran Over A-Bomb."[17] I wonder

17 Steven Weisman, "Bush Aides Divided on Confronting Iran over A-Bomb," *New York Times*, September 21, 2004.

whether Mr. Weisman has information about an A-bomb in Iran, of which the international community is unaware. In the text, Weisman asserted that "Like Iraq in its final years under Saddam Hussein, Iran is believed by experts to be on the verge of developing a nuclear bomb. In Iraq, that proved to be untrue, though this time the consensus is much stronger among Western experts."

I always ask my students to write their sentences in the active tense, passive tenses invite ambiguity and uncertainty and leads your readers to be more skeptical of your assertions. Weisman is no student of mine, but I wonder how his claim stands up to the test of the active reformulation of a sentence. "Iran is believed by experts." Who are these experts? What were the bases of their conclusions that Iran is on the verge of developing a nuclear bomb? Who are the sources of their intelligence? (Not another Chalabi, I hope!) If these "Western experts" were wrong the first time around, what guarantees the validity of their conjectures this time? Weisman adds to the currency of his scenario by offering another piece of intelligence: "Israel also warns that Iran's nuclear program will reach a 'point of no return' next year, after which it will be able to make a bomb without any outside assistance."

Israel's warning appeared in another news piece in the same issue of the *Times*: "Iran Advances Move to Nuclear Fuel, Defying U.N." by Craig Smith.[18] Although Mr. Smith wrote that "Iran has offered to accept any safeguards imposed by the United Nations agency to ensure its enrichment activities," he qualified his report by

18 Craig S. Smith, "Iran Advances Move to Nuclear Fuel, Defying U.N." *New York Times,* September 21, 2004.

reminding the reader, "But some American analysts warn that the international community has only a year or so left to stop the Iranian program from achieving self-sufficiency. After that, they warn, the country will have the means to create a nuclear arsenal without outside help, forever altering the Middle East balance of power." So, in Smith's report, the same piece of intelligence that was provided by "Israel" in Weisman's memo reappears as the warning of "some American analysts." This is, at best, sloppy journalism and, at worst, journalism with an agenda.

The world community should be concerned about the Iranian government's nuclear technology. But on this issue, like in other matters, unilateralism, arrogance, and disengagement will inevitably lead to disaster. It is true that the Iranian government pursues a policy of "altering the balance of power in the Middle East." But after all, this is the same policy that the US promotes and executes. If the Iranians are discontent with the balance of power in the Middle East, such as the open secret of Israel's nuclear weapons, the world community needs to prove that it deals with the question of non-proliferation impartially.

If the US is wary of the intentions of the Islamic Republic, it should follow a policy that renders any hostile policies in Iran irrelevant. It cannot promote regime change and offer financial support to overthrow a sovereign government and expect cooperation at the same time. One cannot invite secrecy and ask for transparency. This policy failed in Iraq, and it will fail in Iran. It will fail in Iran, not only in the context of Iran-US relations, but also in regard to the domestic politics of reform within Iran. American policy, deliberately or unintentionally, promotes a wartime governance in Iran in which every voice of dissent is silenced, and every attempt for democratization is crushed. The reformists in Iran are the biggest losers of a policy the seeds of which were planted by the President when he uttered the words "Axis of Evil."

The nuclear threat is as real as it ever was. Neither selling bunker-buster missiles to Israel, nor threatening the Islamic Republic with a proxy war will deter certain factions in the Iranian government from aspiring to a mature weapons program. Paradoxically, current US policy lends more legitimacy to the Iranian hawks and their ambitions for a nuclear Iran. If the logic of deterrence justified more than fifty years of the nuclear arms race, on what geopolitical grounds could one legitimately ask the Iranian government not to brandish nuclear weapons to deter its regional competitors?

So, what is the solution? Nuclear power plants generate a hazardous amount of radioactive waste, the containment and stabilization of which remains a contentious social and technological problem. Furthermore, these nuclear power plants present to the US and Israel tempting targets for preventive strikes. The Iranian government has already begun its perilous journey to join the nuclear club. It cannot be persuaded to abandon its nuclear power program and adopt renewable energy technologies. From their point of view, green technologies are neither economically sustainable in the short term, nor politically prestigious.

1. As a signatory of the NPT, Iran can legally develop nuclear technology for peaceful purposes. The Iranian government will not voluntarily suspend its legal enrichment program indefinitely. The best solution would be a protocol for technology transfer

from the EU to Iran in exchange for additional international inspection.

2. The Iranian government must demonstrate good will towards the IAEA and the "Big-Three." If it fails to reach a verifiable agreement with the international community, its intransigence will increase the likelihood of Bush's reelection.
3. The US must abandon its ambition for regime change in Iran, no matter who wins the presidential election. America must decouple its nuclear policy from its other concerns regarding Iran's human rights abuses and support of terrorism. Changes in the human rights situation in Iran, and its position on Israel should not be regarded as preconditions for nuclear cooperation. Coupling all three presupposes regime change and thereby forces Iran to abandon the NPT.
4. Non-proliferation cannot be selective. The exemption of Israel from international nuclear treaties undermines the authority of the IAEA. The greatest spur to a regional arms race is Israel's nuclear capabilities. Since nuclear disarmament is not negotiable for Israel, the world community should pressure Israel to fully disclose its weapons program.

The US' pressure to refer Iran's case to the Security Council is premature and misguided. It will only strengthen the position of those on the Iranian side who do not believe in a negotiated settlement. The Iranian daily *Aftab* reported today that the conservative representative of Isfahan in the Parliament announced that he was gathering signatures to introduce a "triple urgent" legislation asking the government to abandon the NPT.

8

Fact, Fiction, and the Politics of a Nuclear Iran

November 2004

The basic thrust of this talk is that the problem of Iran's nuclear technology is a manufactured crisis in line with the American new world order post-communist agenda. Manufactured crises often do turn into real crises with unintended and unplanned consequences, as the case might be in the current row over Iranian nuclear technology. Like any other processes of production, manufacturing crises need conception, raw material, labor, networks of distribution and dissemination, consumption, those who are exploited, and finally, those who benefit from its implications. The Bush administration, Israel, and the European trio (German, France, and Great Britain) have been successful in making the case for the Islamic Republic's "non-compliance" and collapse the Iranian's right under the Non-Proliferation Treaty (NPT) to develop nuclear technology onto the proliferation of nuclear weapons. American mass media, most of which were in compliance with the doctored intelligence on Iraq, once again follows the administration's line on Iran uncritically and disseminate unfounded and ambiguous reports as evidence of another brewing peril from the Middle East.

In a recent investigative piece in the *New York Times* (March 5, 2006), William Broad and David Sanger began their report by raising an alarming question. "When Iran defiantly cut the locks and seals on its nuclear enrichment plants in January and restarted its effort to manufacture atomic fuel, it forced the world to confront a momentous question: How long will it be before Tehran has the ability to produce a bomb that would alter the balance of power in the Middle East?" Although the purpose of Broad and Sanger's piece was to show the technological difficulties that render the development of any weaponized nuclear program far-fetched, they evoke a sense of urgency in their readers' minds by assertions such as "Iran claims that it is racing forward with enrichment." No matter how skeptical the reporting on Iran appears to be, in almost all cases, the non-compliance of Iran and its intention to develop nuclear weapons are treated as given facts.

In the last two years, a large propaganda machinery has been at work to generate, maintain, and escalate this crisis. Just a quick look at the cover pages of a number of recent books on the Iranian nuclear technology-cum-crisis, shows how the infamous mushroom cloud now is originated in Iran. In the view of the mass media, it is the reckless juggling of mullahs with nuclear missiles who now define the most despicable threat to world peace.

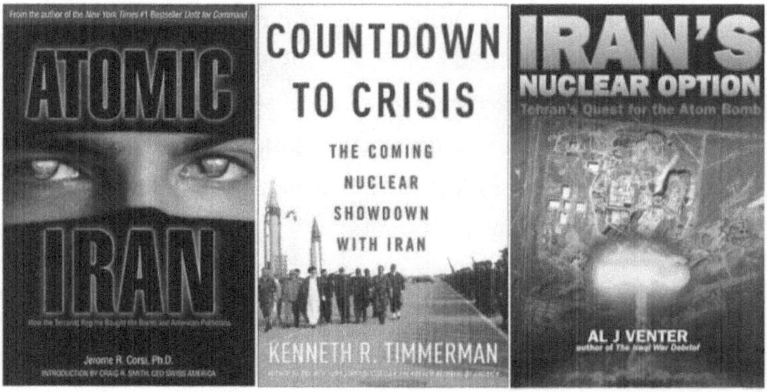

At the core of the controversy over the Iranian nuclear technology lies a simple assertion articulated recently by the Secretary of State Condoleezza Rice that "We may face no greater challenge from a single country than from Iran, whose policies are directed at developing a Middle East that would be 180 degrees different from the Middle East that we would like to see develop. This is a country that is determined, it seems, to develop a nuclear weapon in defiance of the international community..." This contention, often repeated in the mass media as the given fact of the Iranian nuclear technology, is based on a number of false assumptions.

1. Because of its rich oil and natural gas resources, Iran does not need to rely on nuclear technology for its energy production. Therefore, civilian use merely coats the real military agenda behind their pursuit of nuclear technology.
2. The Islamic Republic's mission is to dominate the region, and possibly the world, through its military might and its influence over the global terrorist networks.
3. The Islamic Republic is in defiance of the international community and, as President Bush has repeatedly stated, in "noncompliance" with the international Non-Proliferation Treaty (NPT).

All these suppositions are false.

Does Iran Need Nuclear Technology?

Rather than a question about the Iranian energy sources, whether Iran needs nuclear technology and the capability to enrich uranium poses a political question. Indeed, rather than the problem of "need," the current discourse of nuclear technology frames this question in the context of "rights." *Does Iran have the right to enrich uranium?* That right, of course, is contingent upon the relation between Iran and other members of the nuclear club, and most importantly, with the US. Indeed, as a series of 2003 declassified documents at the National Security Archives disclosed, the Ford Administration encouraged the Shah of Iran to consider a large investment (up to 23 nuclear reactors) in nuclear technology.[19]

Iran, which was one of the first signatories of the NPT agreement in 1968, pursued the plan with signing a contract with Kraftwerk Union (a subsidiary of the German Siemens) to construct two light-water reactors in Bushehr, a Persian Gulf port city. In 1975, MIT signed a contract with the Iranian government to establish an education and training program for Iranian scientists and engineers. During the same year, the US Secretary of State Henry Kissinger, had signed National Security Decision Memorandum 292, titled "US-Iran Nuclear Cooperation," which laid out the details of the sale of nuclear energy equipment to Iran projected to bring US corporations more than $6 billion in revenue. At the time, Iran was pumping as much as 6 million barrels of oil a day, compared with an average of about 4 million barrels daily today.

President Gerald R. Ford even signed a directive in 1976 offering Tehran the chance to buy and operate a US-built reprocessing facility for extracting plutonium from nuclear reactor fuel. The deal was for a complete "nuclear fuel cycle." The Ford strategy paper stated that the "introduction of nuclear power will both provide for the

---

19 For a detailed account of the history of the nuclear technology in Iran, see Mohammad Sahimi, "Forced to Fuel: Iran's Nuclear Energy Program," *Harvard International Review,* vol. 26, no. 4, 2005, pp. 42-45.

growing needs of Iran's economy and free remaining oil reserves for export or conversion to petrochemicals."

By 1978, only seven months prior to the collapse of the Pahlavi monarchy in Iran, the final draft of the US-Iran Nuclear Energy Agreement, which envisioned the construction of 8 nuclear reactors, was signed. This was in addition to other French and German agreements for the establishment of the Iranian nuclear energy infrastructure.

After the revolution in February 1979, the Provisional government cancelled these contracts, except for the Bushehr reactor, and decided to divert its financial resources to other infrastructural needs. At the time, the Bushehr reactor was more than 90 percent complete and the Germans had agreed to finish the project and begin enrichment in less than two years. In the summer of 1980, the Iraqi forces invaded Southwest of Iran. The Iraqi air force destroyed much of the two plants in Bushehr and thereby returned Iran to its pre-nuclear period.

The point of this history is to demonstrate the historical inconsistencies in the argument often put forward by the Administration that Iran's *energy* "needs" does not justify its nuclear ambitions. The US abandoned its own "need-based" argument of the 1970s by discounting the Iranian energy predicament in favor of its nuclear weapons ambitions. So long as the Shah of Iran, by no account a democratic regime but a friend of the US of A, was in power, Iran needed nuclear technology to sustain its sources of energy. With the collapse of the monarchy in 1979, gone was the Iranians' right and their need to develop nuclear technology. With the recent nuclear cooperation agreement with India, it has become evident that, as the conservative columnist David Brooks recently observed, the entire legal and political frame of nuclear technology directly depends on the "nature of the regimes, stupid."

What Are the Islamic Republic's Global Strategies?

Henry Precht, the former Director of the Iranian Affairs of the State Department (1978-1980), aptly captured the core of the argument when he wrote that "the immediate agenda of the Islamic Republic's leaders is political and economic independence at home, not dominion abroad."[20] In its more than quarter-of-a-century history, the Islamic Republic has shown that despite its ideological propensities, it is a regime based on strong pragmatic concerns for its own survival. From its perpetual domestic negotiations on reconciling Islam with the expediencies of state policies, to Ayatollah Khomeini's famous admission of "drinking chalice of poison" in accepting the UN Resolution 598 to end the Iran-Iraq war, the Islamic regime has been consistent in its determination to choose its own immediate interest over any transcendental fantasies of world domination.

Particularly after the collapse of the Soviet Union and the first Gulf War, the Islamic regime became more aware of its military and political vulnerability against American interests in the region. Since 1991, the Islamic Republic has pursued a double-edged policy of

---

20 Henry Precht, "Ayatollah Realpolitik," *Foreign Policy,* no. 70 (Spring, 1988), pp, 109-128.

appeasement as well as tough rhetoric in its relationship with the US. While the Iranian domestic politics determines the degree of the distribution of the two parts of this policy, all Iranian administrations have remained open, if not overtly, to the idea of the normalization of relations with the US.

After September 11, 2001, the Khatami Administration in Iran seized the opportunity to engage with its American counterpart in bringing the perpetrators of the terrorist act to justice. As reported by Flynt Leverett, then senior director for Middle East affairs in the National Security Council (NSC), in meetings with Bush administration officials in Paris and Geneva, the Iranians offered to help unseat the Taliban government in Afghanistan and assist the American forces in any possible operations in the region. Iranians also agreed to exert pressure on their own allies in Afghanistan, the Northern Alliance, to accept the Americans' choice for the interim government after the collapse of the Taliban regime. James Dobbins, then the US special envoy to Afghanistan, recalled that Iran played a "decisive role" in persuading the Northern Alliance delegates to compromise at the Bonn Conference to determine the future government of Afghanistan. Iranians even went further to make sure that the language of "war on terrorism" was included in the agreement. Furthermore, the Khatami administration agreed to amass the Iranian Army along the Afghan borders to assist US military missions and prevent members of Al-Qa'eda from crossing over into Iran.[21]

21 For a detailed report, see: Mark Fields and Ramsha Ahmed, "A Review of the 2001 Bonn Conference and Application to the Road Ahead in Afghanistan,"

Under the influence of the Defense Policy Board of the Pentagon, after the initial cooperation and the successful transition of power to the interim government of Hamid Karzai, the Bush White House rejected the Islamic Republic's rapprochement *in toto*. In early 2002, a secret Pentagon report to Congress on its "Nuclear Posture Review" named Iran as one of the seven countries against which nuclear weapons might be used "in the event of surprising military developments."[22] Five days later, Pres. Bush referred to Iran in his State of the Union address as being part of an "axis of evil," along with Iraq and North Korea. "By seeking weapons of mass destruction," he said, "these regimes pose a grave and growing danger."

Two principals have guided the Bush Administration's position on Iran's nuclear ambitions. The first is an ideological conviction that bestows a historical responsibility onto the US to reconstitute the world after its own image. The second is a doctrinal approach in which the American defense policy and strategic threat assessment stress capability and military technological capacity over intention and the *realpolitik* of its adversaries. Both of these principles inevitably contribute to the dominance of a view that constructs the Islamic Republic as *inherently* and *irrationally* anti-US, and therefore unquestionably determined in its deadly campaign against American interests. None of the American threat assessments address the

Institute for National Strategic Studies, 2001. Accessible at https://inss.ndu.edu/Portals/68/Documents/stratperspective/inss/Strategic-Perspectives-8.pdf

22 The report was obtained by defense analyst William Arkin, who revealed its contents in the Los Angeles Times on Jan 26, 2002.

question *why* Iran should launch a nuclear attack on Israel or any of the European nations, knowing that such an attack will inevitably lead to their own annihilation. In that context, the Islamic Republic acts like a suicide bomber, who does not respect life, and is not deterred by death. To thwart Iran from acquiring nuclear technology, it is necessary to construe the Iranian regime as ideological, irrational, and self-destructive.

In none of its stated positions, the administration gives any weight to the *Iranian's* threat assessment and how it might relate to their nuclear ambition. Recently, two former CIA officials, who were directly involved in producing estimates on Iran, revealed in separate interviews that the National Intelligence Estimates on Iran have consistently portrayed its concerns about the military threat posed by the US as a central consideration in Tehran's pursuit of a nuclear weapon capability. Paul Pillar, who managed the writing of all NIEs on Iran from 2000 to 2005 as the national intelligence officer for the Near East and South Asia, argued that "all of the NIEs on Iran during that period addressed the Iranian fears of US attack explicitly and related their desire for nuclear weapons to those fears."[23]

See Map 1 (2002) and Map 2 (2005) and compare the increase in American military presence along the Iranian borders

23 https://en.wikinews.org/wiki/Newspaper_alleges_U.S._drawing_up_plans_to_attack_Iran

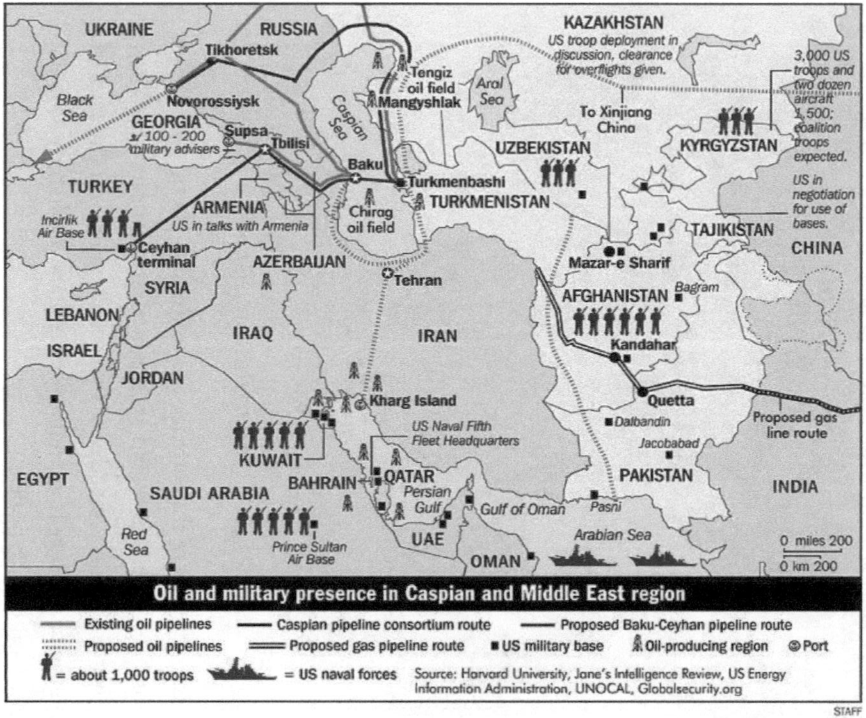
UKRAINE
RUSSIA
Tikhoretsk
Black Sea
Novorossiysk
GEORGIA
100 - 200 military advisers
Supsa
Tbilisi
Caspian Sea
Tengiz oil field
Mangyshlak
Aral Sea
KAZAKHSTAN
US troop deployment in discussion, clearance for overflights given.
To Xinjiang China
3,000 US troops and two dozen aircraft
1,500: coalition troops expected.
KYRGYZSTAN
UZBEKISTAN
Baku
Turkmenbashi
TURKMENISTAN
TURKEY
ARMENIA
US in talks with Armenia
Incirlik Air Base
Chirag oil field
US in negotiation for use of bases.
TAJIKISTAN
CHINA
Ceyhan terminal
AZERBAIJAN
Tehran
Mazar-e Sharif
SYRIA
AFGHANISTAN
Bagram
LEBANON
IRAQ
IRAN
ISRAEL
Kandahar
JORDAN
Kharg Island
Quetta
Dalbandin
Proposed gas line route
US Naval Fifth Fleet Headquarters
Jacobabad
KUWAIT
EGYPT
BAHRAIN
QATAR
PAKISTAN
INDIA
SAUDI ARABIA
Persian Gulf
Gulf of Oman
Pasni
Red Sea
Prince Sultan Air Base
UAE
OMAN
Arabian Sea
0 miles 200
0 km 200
Oil and military presence in Caspian and Middle East region
Existing oil pipelines
Caspian pipeline consortium route
Proposed Baku-Ceyhan pipeline route
Proposed oil pipelines
Proposed gas pipeline route
US military base
Oil-producing region
Port
= about 1,000 troops
= US naval forces
Source: Harvard University, Jane's Intelligence Review, US Energy Information Administration, UNOCAL, Globalsecurity.org
STAFF

Map 1. 2002

Map 2, 2005 (Oxford Research Group)

The dominant view of the intelligence community in the past three years has been that Iran would seek a nuclear weapons capability, but analysts have also considered that a willingness on the part of Washington to reassure Iran on its security fears would have a significant effect on Iranian policy.

The Bush administration, however, has been moving towards the opposite direction. It insists on its contradictory policy of pressuring

Iran to open its facilities for unconditional inspection of international monitors, on the one hand, and on other hand, publicly announces and sets aside a budget for regime change in Iran. In mid-February, President Bush asked Congress to authorize an extra $75 million to help the US spur democracy in Iran. That is in addition to the $10 million already used so far in 2006. In addition to the line-item budget in Congress, a recently unclassified State Department document shows that the Bush administration quietly orchestrated a major shift in US policy towards Iran.[24] The document reveals that the administration actively pursues plans to topple the Islamic Republic and has set aside $85 million to establish offices in the region, in Dubai, Turkey, Azerbaijan. The plan calls for hiring Farsi-speaking agents to operate a network of intelligence gathering and an anti-government propaganda machine. "Our model," the document declares, "is Riga Station that the United States maintained in the USSR and provided diplomats (like George Kennan) with everyday practice in Russian language and culture." Now that the State Department has transformed the United Arab Emirates into the Baltic States and Dubai into Riga, they also need to be mindful that only 10 percernt of Riga reports were accurate.

Beyond its confrontational rhetoric, which often is designed for domestic consumption or regional politics, the Islamic Republic follows a definite pragmatic international policy. The history of the Islamic regime shows very well that their intervention in global Islamic causes and their involvement in the Palestinian-Israeli

24 https://images1.americanprogress.org/il80web20037/ThinkProgress/2006/0293_001.pdf

conflict is often informed by their own national security interests and their own issues of sovereignty. The more secure they feel in their own land, the less they incline to pose a threat abroad.

Is Iran in Violation of the NPT?

The Islamic Republic endeavored to revive its nuclear technology program in 1982 when the Rafsanjani government approached Kraftwerk Union to complete the Bushehr project. The United States, which at the time was supporting Saddam Hussein's war efforts against Iran, pressured the German government to stop Kraftwerk from delivering any nuclear technology to Iran. The $5.4 billion-dollar lawsuit is still pending in the International Commerce Commission.

The Islamic regime approached a number of other countries, from Argentina to Spain and France, in the open market to acquire nuclear technology and know-how. In each case the US threatened the countries approached by Iran with sanctions and economic retaliation. Finally, Iran signed a contract with Russia for the completion of Bushehr and another with China for the purchase of uranium hexafluoride (used for uranium enrichment) in 1991. These contracts were all within the NPT and under IAEA safeguards.

The Iranian government also engaged in a clandestine operation for building a large underground processing facility in Natanz. They purchased the equipment in the nuclear black market and almost completed the plant with indigenous scientists and some creative technological problem-solving. The government launched its clandestine underground as well as its open official nuclear program, with the anticipation of military strikes against its facilities. They carefully decentralized them and dispersed the reactor, processing, and mining sites throughout the country.

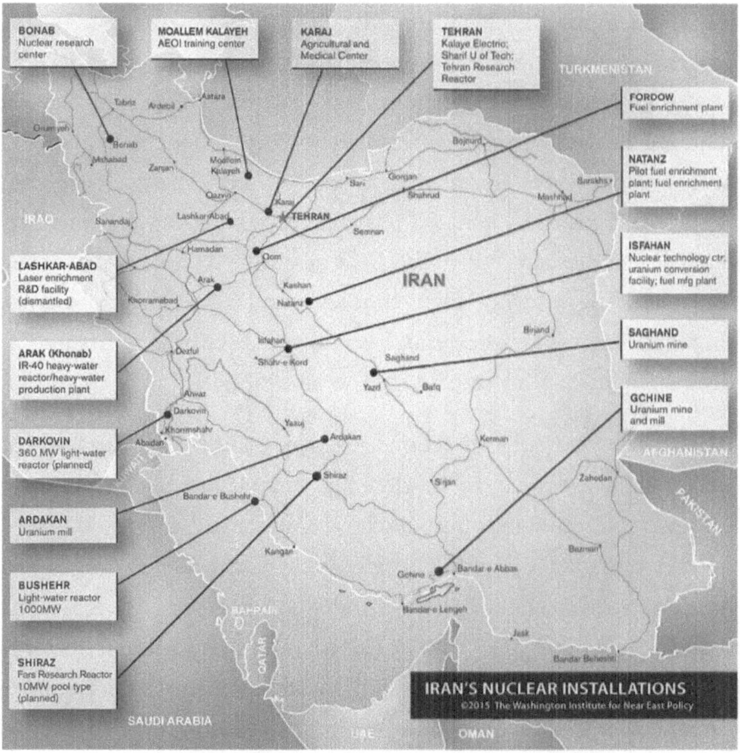

In 2002, the People's Mujahedin Organization, a group on the state department's terrorist list, exposed the Islamic regime's clandestine operations and revealed the location of the Natanz processing plant. Even at the time, however, Iran was not in breach of its NPT obligations. According to the original IAEA safeguard agreements, Iran was obliged to report the plant's activities 180 days before introducing any nuclear material.

Nevertheless, the appearance of a clandestine operation was enough for the international community to pressure Iran to take concrete "confidence-building measures." In August 2003, Iran reached an agreement with the EU3, France-Germany-Great Britain, in Paris to sign an Additional Protocol with the IAEA. The Paris agreement required Iran to suspend voluntarily its enrichment activities and accept an intrusive regime of "snap inspections." Furthermore, Iran agreed to the IAEA's demand to install recording cameras in all its nuclear facilities. In return, the EU3 guaranteed to recognize Iran's inalienable right to nuclear technology under the NPT and work on technological assistance and economic incentives to assure the peaceful nature of the Iranian nuclear ambitions.

After three years of inspections, even of military facilities which were not included in the original agreement, the IAEA found no evidence of a military component in the Iranian nuclear program. Indeed, on January 31, 2006, the IAEA Updated Brief stated: "Iran has continued to facilitate access under its Safeguards Agreement as requested by the Agency and has acted as if the Additional Protocol is in force, including by providing in a timely manner the requisite declarations and access locations." Four days later, on February 4, the IAEA board approved the referral of Iran to the UN Security Council. The board argued that Iran has failed to show the peaceful nature of its nuclear program. Under pressure from the US government, the IAEA board changed the main objective of the Additional Protocol from finding evidence of "any diversion of nuclear material to nuclear weapons or other nuclear explosive devices," which it had found none, to "finding proof of its exclusive civilian use."

To avoid referral to the UN Security Council and to defuse the coming crisis, three days before its February 4 meeting, the Islamic Republic submitted a six-point proposal to the IAEA board. The EU3 and the US shunned the proposal as irrelevant and refused to consider it. The media did not report the content of the proposal that could potentially avert the escalation of the crisis. In their six-point document, the Iranian side proposed

- Iran pledges that its nuclear program is for peaceful purposes, not nuclear bombs.
- Iran pledges that it will get the legislative approval in its majlis (parliament) of the Additional Protocol to the nuclear Non-Proliferation Treaty (NPT) and will continue with IAEA inspections.
- Iran pledges to stay within the NPT.
- Iran pledges that it will not resume enrichment prior to the next IAEA meeting.
- Iran pledges that its nuclear research will be under monitoring by the IAEA.
- Iran will continue negotiating with the EU-3 regarding enrichment issues for two years, and after two years, if the negotiations fail, will resume enrichment activities.

Double Standards

It appears that the NPT has lost its utility in a world that is governed by what the Iranian government has termed a nuclear apartheid. No document has been produced and no evidence has been generated to indicate Iran's noncompliance. Meanwhile, serious violators of the NPT, including the US, and the non-signatories of the NPT, India, Pakistan, and Israel, remain unchallenged by the IAEA and the UN Security Council.

The Islamic Republic could be the author of three scenarios: first the Iranian leaders might be sincere in their stated goal of civilian use of their nuclear technology; second they might be buying time to develop a full scale nuclear arsenal and use that as a deterrent against hostile forces; three, they might intend to gain the scientific know-how and technological capability of weapons grade enrichment, but reserve the option of its actual production. I believe the most likely scenario is the third and that is why the best policy to dissuade the Islamic Republic from the militarization of its nuclear technology is engaged negotiations and security guarantees by the US. So long as the Islamic Republic perceives itself under siege, it will uphold the option of the militarization of its nuclear program.

As Joseph Cirincione, a non-proliferation specialist at the Carnegie Endowment for International Peace, observed, an analysis that links Iran's security concerns about the US to its quest for nuclear weapons would be consistent with the history of other nations' policies toward acquiring nuclear weapons. "No nation has ever been coerced into giving up a nuclear program," he said, "but many have been convinced to do so by the disappearance of the threat."

9

Whose Justice Does Saddam's Trial Serve?

October 2005

In a quiet neighborhood of the Tajrish district of Tehran, on the foothills of the Alborz Mountains, a green thirty-thousand-square-foot sanatorium hosts hundreds of veterans of the Iran-Iraq war who still suffer from their war wounds. The majority of these veterans have resided in Asayeshagh Sarollah, only one of numerous sanatoria throughout the country, since the early days of the war, which began in the summer of 1980, lasted for eight years, and claimed the lives of one million people on both sides. The residents of Sarollah count for a fraction of the estimated 100,000 victims of chemical weapons used by the Iraqi regime during the eight-year war. These "living martyrs," as they came to be known in Iran, are the forgotten soldiers of a war without winners.

A reporter from *Sharq,* a Tehran daily, wrote recently that during a visit to the sanatorium, Mr. Mohseni, a twenty-year resident, pulled him aside, making sure that they were away from the eyes of the keepers, and whispered in his ears, "Up to last year, the country used to celebrate Veterans Week, this year we observed Veterans Day, soon we're going have just a moment of silence in honor of the dead." With Saddam Hussein's trial underway in Baghdad, many Iranian victims of his aggression hope that "finally the world will hear," as one paraplegic veteran muttered to the *Sharq* reporter, "our story."

As it happens, the world will not hear their stories during Hussein's trial. The invasion of Iran is missing from the twelve counts of indictment against the former dictator, and evidence and testimony about the atrocities carried out under his command will not be presented to the court. The conspicuous absence of his war crimes against Iranian civilians, and his widespread use of chemical weapons from 1982 to the final days of the war in 1988, raises serious questions about the objectives of this trial. Sweeping Hussein's atrocities against Iranian citizens under the courtroom rug could only mean that this trial is more about a political theatre for the legitimacy of the new regime and its American backers, than a genuine thirst for justice.

In September of 1980, Saddam Hussein invaded the province of Khuzestan, in southwest Iran and launched air and rocket attacks against major Iranian cities. The invasion led to one of the longest-running full-blown wars of the last century between the two countries. Since even the former UN Secretary General Javier Perez de Cuellar declared Iraq in 1991 the aggressor in the war, it remains bewildering that Hussein is not going to be tried for his crimes against Iranians. He ordered the use of chemical weapons against

Iranian soldiers and revolutionary militia, approved the indiscriminate bombing of Iranian cities, and for eight years targeted city neighborhoods with long-range SCUD missiles.

The Iraqi judiciary has announced that the twelve counts of the indictment were put together for cases that had documented and unambiguous evidence. But this is true of the Iran-Iraq war. There is no dearth of documentation—from satellite photos of the use of chemical weapons to living survivors of these attacks, all could easily be presented in a court of law. What this trial lacks is political will on the part of the US, the Iraqi government, and the Islamic Republic to bring forth these charges.

The Americans have the most at stake in this trial. Not only is the White House trying to use the proceedings as yet another justification for the overthrow of Hussein and the invasion of Iraq, but the Bush administration also intends to conceal the misguided policies of its predecessors, especially during the Iran-Iraq war. Indicting Hussein for his Iran-Iraq war crimes will inevitably raise questions about the role of the US in encouraging and lending support to his war machine. As declassified documents, published by the National Security Archive, from the Reagan Administration clearly indicate, from 1980 to 1984, the US government steadily provided political, intelligence, and military support for Hussein's regime. Reagan officials believed that the Iraqi invasion would contain the Islamic revolution and would thereby block its "domino effect" in the region. For example, in an April 8, 1981, cable from Secretary of State Alexander Haig to the United States Interest Section in Iraq (at the time, the US did not have full diplomatic relations with Iraq), the Secretary sent a personal message to Sa'adun Hammadi, the Iraqi Minister of Foreign Affairs, noting that it is important that "our two countries be able to exchange views, freely and on a systematic basis." This message initiated a long series of negotiations and high-level visits between Baghdad and Washington, throughout the Iran-Iraq war, and eventually led to the restoration of full diplomatic relations between the two governments.[25]

By early 1982, American support for Hussein's regime intensified after Iran deflected the invasion and forced Iraqi troops back across the border into a defensive position. Measures already underway to upgrade US-Iraqi relations were accelerated, and in February 1982, the State Department removed Iraq from its list of states supporting international terrorism. The decision was made after the US's own intelligence reported the massive use of chemical weapons by the Iraqi forces against Iranian "human wave" offensives. In spite of congressional objections, the Reagan administration's rehabilitation of Iraq lifted barriers for direct military and technological aid to Hussein's regime. American corporations exported helicopters, dual-use insecticides, and the Department of Defense shared intelligence with Hussein's regime about the Iranian army's strategic positions.

Officials from the State Department's Bureau of Politico-Military Affairs informed Secretary Shultz of the additional information they had acquired on Iraqis' "almost daily" use of chemical weapons. In March 1983, they noted, "We also know that Iraq has acquired a CW [chemical weapons] capability, presumably from Western firms, including possibly a US foreign subsidiary." Meanwhile,

25 https://nsarchive2.gwu.edu/NSAEBB/NSAEBB82/#docs

on December 20, 1983, Donald Rumsfeld, then special envoy for President Reagan, traveled to Baghdad and met Saddam Hussein without raising any concerns about his war crimes (see their infamous handshake in the video clip on the National Security Archive link). In March 1984, the Islamic Republic introduced a draft resolution to the UN Security Council condemning Iraq's use of chemical weapons. The State Department instructed the US delegate to the United Nations to get the support of other Western missions for a motion of "no decision" regarding Iran's draft resolution. The US successfully campaigned to block the Security Council from naming Iraq in its final resolution against the use of chemical weapons.

In light of this history, shouldn't the Iraqi court hold US policymakers accountable for their support of Hussein's war crimes? Shouldn't the misguided policy of proxy wars against whomever the US government deems its enemy be tried in this court?

Why doesn't the Islamic Republic take its case to the court? The Islamic Republic follows a policy of appeasement towards the post Saddam Hussein government of Iraq. Although, as recently as last week, the Iranian Minister of Justice, Ayatollah Shahroudi, announced that they would submit charges against Hussein to the court, all the players in the political scene of the two countries know that the angry press conferences in Tehran are for domestic consumption. The Iranian government does not intend to demand reparations from the new regime in Iraq for the destruction and misery the war inflicted on its citizens. As an editorial in the daily English language *Iran News* stressed recently, despite the fact that UN Resolution 598 (by which Iran agreed to a cease-fire) expressly stated that Iran was entitled to billions of dollars of war reparations, the Iranian Ministry of Foreign Affairs has been indecisive and ineffectual in pursuing its rightful reparation claims.

While maintaining good relations with the new regime in Iraq might explain one side of the Islamic Republic's reluctance to pursue criminal charges against Hussein, the other pertinent factor is the question of why the Iranian side continued fighting the war after they repelled the initial Iraqi invasion. This is a question that is revisited every year at the anniversary of the Iraqi attack, a question the answer to which might point to questionable dealings and war profiteering among Iranian government officials. Introducing additional indictments on the Iran-Iraq war might result in calls for an investigation into the reasons for perpetuating the war for another six years, when a peace agreement was feasible after Hussein's forces were fended off in 1982. Who made what decisions, when and why are not quite the type of questions the Iranian side would like to see explored during Hussein's trial.

The Iranian victims of Hussein's brutality deserve justice. Let this justice lead to the indictment of the tunnel vision, short-sided, and one-dimensional American foreign policy, or shed light on the role of those who prolonged the Iran-Iraq war. Those who make decisions to commit murder, corporations which benefit from destruction, and policymakers who tried their best to shield Hussein at the height of his atrocities from the censure of the international community, should join him at the seat of the accused!

10

Chemical Hypocrisy

September 2013

On August 26, 2013 Secretary of State John Kerry gave a rare and pointed speech in which he sent a clear message to the Syrian regime. "What we saw last week in Syria," referring to the use of chemical weapons, "should shock the conscience of the world, it defies any code of morality… It is a moral obscenity." Barely able to contain his outrage, Kerry reminded the world that "This is about the large-scale, indiscriminate use of weapons that the civilized world long ago decided must never be used at all – a conviction shared even by countries that agree on little else."[26]

Earlier on that very same day, *Foreign Policy* published an exclusive investigative report that showed for the first time how the CIA helped Saddam Hussein as he gassed Iranian troops and civilians

26 https://www.youtube.com/watch?v=So1T1HdDpJw

from 1983-1988.[27] The fact that the US and Western European powers, particularly Germany, France, and Italy, assisted Hussein during the bloody eight-year war with Iran is not new. It has been known that Western powers saw in Hussein's aggression against Iran an opportunity to contain the Iranian revolution from spreading in the Arab and Islamic world. They provided intelligence to the Iraqi side in addition to hundreds of millions of dollars worth of military hardware, from tanks to jet fighters.

What is new in *Foreign Policy's* report is that it is based on the recently declassified CIA documents that clearly show that the Reagan Administration was not only aware of, but encouraged Iraq's use of chemical weapons. The documents show that rather than stopping Saddam Hussein from the use of chemical weapons, the CIA's main concern was stopping Iran from acquiring hard evidence to prove that Iraq had used chemical weapons.

A top-secret CIA document from November 1983 reported that "As Iraqi attacks continue and intensify the chances increase that Iranian forces will acquire a shell containing mustard agent with Iraqi markings. Tehran would take such evidence to the U.N. and charge US complicity in violating international law." President Ronald Reagan even dispatched special envoy to the Middle East, Donald Rumsfeld to deliver his assurances that the US would continue to support Hussein's war efforts. Unfortunately (for Rumsfeld), that

27 Shane Harris and Matthew M. Aid, "America Helped Saddam as He Gassed Iran," *Foreign Policy*, August 26, 2013.

visit is now a part of the public record along with that infamous handshake with Hussein in December 1983.

Iran made two unsuccessful attempts during the war to present its case against Hussein to the United Nations Security Council. The documents further show that the US had meticulously detailed the use of the CW by the Hussein regime, but cynically rejected the Iranians' claim because they failed to offer "persuasive evidence of the weapons' use."

The documents (see a series of passages below) show how "the United States," as the authors of the *Foreign Policy* article assert, "applied a cold calculus three decades ago to Saddam Hussein's widespread use of chemical weapons against his enemies, who at the time were and still are our enemies, and his own people. The Reagan administration decided that it was better to let the attacks continue if they might turn the tide of the war."

Toward the end of 1987, the Iranian side began a massive buildup around the Iraqi borders, planning the capture of the strategic city of Basra. The Department of Defense analysts were doubtful that the Iraqi side could withstand such a massive attack and believed that the fall of Basra was near. They were also convinced that with the fall of Basra, the Iraqi military would collapse and Iran would win the war.

A report entitled "At the Gate of Basra" was presented to Reagan, warning him of the imminent danger of Iraq's defeat. By this time, the Reagan administration was fully aware of the Iraqi regime's massive use of mustard gas, sarin, and Tabun nerve agent (also known as GA) against Iranian troops and civilians. Despite that full awareness, on the margins of the report, President Reagan wrote a note addressed to Secretary of Defense Frank Carlucci: "An Iranian victory is unacceptable."

Throughout the eight-year war, the Iranian regime maintained a position against the use of chemical weapons. They remained committed to their international and humanitarian obligations and refused to develop or to use weapons of mass destruction, even during those days when retaliating in kind against Iraqi aggressors appeared quite tempting. Iran remains true to this position and has never developed a chemical weapons program.

One of the main justifications President Obama presented in his September 10, 2013 address on why the US must act against Syria was that if we don't, it will embolden Iran. "A failure to stand against the use of chemical weapons," he pleaded, "would weaken prohibitions against other weapons of mass destruction and embolden Assad's ally, Iran, which must decide whether to ignore international law by building a nuclear weapon or to take a more peaceful path."

It would be helpful for Obama to pause for a second and reflect on his comment. When the US deemed the defeat of Hussein plausible, his predecessors and his allies supplied and covered up the use of chemical weapons to save the Iraqi regime. They worried that "any publicity about Iraq's widespread use of chemical weapons could set back recent efforts to strengthen Iraqi-US ties."

"Terrible things happen across the globe," the US President opined, "and it is beyond our means to right every wrong, but when with modest effort and risk we can stop children from being gassed to death and thereby make our own children safer over the long run, I believe we should act," Obama said near the conclusion of his address. "That's what makes America different. That's what makes us exceptional. With humility, but with resolve, let us never lose sight of that essential truth."

The terrible thing about what the President says is that we know that there is nothing essential about the truth that informs American policies abroad. One thing that the recent CIA documents about the Iran-Iraq war make clear is the instrumental use of truth in American policy. There might be a case for American exceptionalism, but that case most definitely is not defined by the American commitment to any essential truth and unwavering defense of human dignity.

Is the conscience of the Secretary of State disturbed by the release of these declassified documents? Is there any moral outrage or an ethical crisis in the White House that chemical weapons were used in order to advance the interests of the US in the Middle East only thirty years ago? (Let us not talk about the use of depleted uranium in Iraq now.)

In a perfect world, Obama would have appeared in front of the cameras and would tell the world that the recent declassified documents show that we had made a terrible error. We supported a regime that used weapons of mass destruction and helped that regime to hide its atrocities. We have learned from this past transgression and seek a better future. We commend Iran for showing restraint and for remaining principled during the war with Iraq by refusing to retaliate against Hussein with chemical weapons. Today Iran should play its crucial role in stopping the use of chemical weapons in Syria. Iranians paid a grave price when the "civilized" world remained silent against the atrocities of Saddam Hussein during the eight-year war. They must be a part of the solution in Syria, especially now that the chemical weapons have been introduced in the theater of this savage war.

11

A Paradigm Shift in the Middle East: Iran as the Solution, Not the Problem

February 2017

A well-orchestrated alliance emerged against Iran during last week's Munich Security Conference. The stage was set by Mike Pence after he called Tehran "the leading state sponsor of terrorism and accused the Islamic Republic of continuing to "destabilize the Middle East." Further, to reiterate the Trumps administration's dissatisfaction with Obama's policy toward Iran, he speculated that with "the end of nuclear-related sanctions, Iran now has additional resources to devote to these efforts."

One after another, representatives of Saudi Arabia, Israel, and, surprisingly, Turkey added their warnings about the rise of the Iranian menace and called for a united front to combat Iranian regional and global ambitions. The Saudi Foreign Minister, Adel al-Jubeir told delegates at the conference "Iran remains the single main sponsor of terrorism in the world." Iran is, he said, "determined to upend the order in the Middle East." In an act more reminiscent of a scene from a theater of the absurd, the Israeli Defense Minister, Avigdor Lieberman, declared "Iran had an ultimate objective of undermining Saudi Arabia in the Middle East." He called for a multilateral dialogue with Sunni Arab states to defeat Iran and its "radical" elements in the region. This was not the first time that the Saudi and Israeli positions on the Middle East security coincided, but the similarities in the way Lieberman and al-Jubeir articulated their grievances against Iran, using the exact same language in listing Iranian transgressions was unprecedented.

Rather bewildering was the Turkish foreign minister, Mevlüt Çavuşoğlu, who added his voice of discontent with Iran and joined in the same vein to call for a concerted international effort against what he termed "an Iranian sectarian policy to undermine Bahrain and Saudi Arabia." He told a friendly audience in Munich that Turkey will not tolerate divisive religious or sectarian policies and, he continued, "we are now normalizing our relations with Israel." Çavuşoğlu's address was particularly baffling since it came following a complex series of negotiations and an agreement that was reached earlier this month between Russia, Turkey and Iran for a cooperation to end Syria's bloody civil war.

The Trump administration and a significant number of lawmakers, Republicans and Democrats, will almost certainly use the display of unity among regional powers against the Islamic Republic to justify new sanctions on Iran. But why, despite the clear evidence to the contrary, are the US and its allies in the region holding Iran solely responsible for destabilizing the Middle East? There are two, one geopolitical and the other purely economic, reasons for such a flagrant distortion of realities on the ground.

From the early days of the Iranian revolution in 1979, the main strategic interest of the US and its corrupt Arab allies has been to fend off the Iranian ambition of exporting its revolution. At the time, it was the stated purpose of the Islamic Republic to spread the message of what they believed to be the Islam of the downtrodden abroad. Almost four decades later, surviving an eight-year war with Saddam Hussein, which he fought on behalf of the concerned Arab nations (with the exception of Syria) and their Western supporters, consolidating power by eliminating most opposition forces inside the country, and managing a beleaguered economy plagued with ongoing regimes of sanctions, the Islamic Republic has been transformed. At the end of the war with Iraq, it became evident that the mantra that the regime in Tehran now followed, as Henry Precht, the former head of the State Department's Iran desk, once said, was not dominion abroad, but economic and political independence at home. Rather than an irrational ideological fervor, the Islamic Republic's policies are primarily motivated by domestic stability, security, and economic growth. Iran has always been more sympathetic to the Christian Armenia than to Muslim Azerbaijan in their border disputes, more interested in closer ties with India than Pakistan, and in order to protect their trade relations with China, remained silent when the Chinese violently suppressed the grievances of their Muslims.

Domestically, Iran has also changed significantly since the brutal years of the 1980s reign of terror. There exists a vibrant and growing civil society, more than fifteen independent newspapers are published in Tehran, meaningful presidential and parliamentary elections with real participation and rivalries happen, unlike a commonplace perception, women participate in social life despite patriarchal laws and cultures, more than 60 percent of university students are women. I do not intend to draw a rosy picture of Iran, the Islamic Republic is not a democratic regime, but in all cases it is certainly more democratic than all our allies in the region.

Oil is not the only rationale that defines our economic interest in the Middle East. Since the end of the Cold War, the US arms sales in the Middle East have been rising exponentially. As a recent report by Stockholm International Peace Research Institute shows, more than half of the total US arms export goes to the Middle East.[28] During the last four years, the sales of arms to the Middle East have doubled. Saudi Arabia's arms import has increased 212 percent from 2012 to 2016. During the same period, Qatar's import of weapons surged 245 percent. Saudi Arabia spends 25 percent of its budget, $85 billion a year, more than that of Russia, on defense. Last year, the Obama administration approved a $38 billion military aid package to Israel for the next ten years. One-third of the world's arms deals happen in the Middle East. All this happens when Iran uses only 2.5 percent of its national budget on defense and relies mostly on domestic production of weapons rather than on a shopping spree in the global arms market.

---

28 https://www.sipri.org/media/press-release/2017/increase-arms-transfers-driven-demand-middle-east-and-asia-says-sipri

A military-industrial complex has taken American foreign policy hostage. It has colonized American foreign policy through a marketing strategy that perpetuates hostilities and generates animosity between different nations. It has promoted an arms race, particularly in the Middle East, that is draining the resources of nations around the world and is weighing heavily on the shoulders of American taxpayers. Military aid to our allies in the region is nothing but a transfer of wealth from ordinary Americans to defense contractors. None of these sales and aid packages would be justifiable if it were not for the existence of an enemy such as the Islamic Republic of Iran reproduced in Pence's caricature, an irrational, ideological nemesis that does not respond to conventional deterrence and needs to be forced into submission to our demands.

Washington needs to transcend its old-age reliance on allies in the Middle East whose interests are increasingly becoming detrimental to peace and stability in the region. The problem in the Middle East is not about Sunni and Shi'ite rivalry, it is not even about Israeli and Palestinian existential animosity. What plagues the Middle East is the narrow-mindedness of its ruling elites, both elected and self-appointed, who have failed to represent and safeguard the interests of their own people. Since the end of WWII, Washington's policy has been exclusively based on securing the economic and geo-political interests of American energy and military industrial corporations. The time has come for the US to rethink its alignment with old patriarchal powers and to look beyond its narrow economic interests in the rising arms race in the Middle East. Extending and expanding sanctions against Iran would be an irreversible step toward opening a new war front, one with broader and more catastrophic consequences around the world.

12

The East-Bound Wind Causes a Storm in the West: Iran-China Sign Long-Term Trade Agreement

July 2020

A few months after the publication of his remarkable book, *Adam Smith in Beijing*,[29] I had an illuminating conversation with Giovanni Arrighi about the significance of China in world history. The late sociologist was interested in knowing more about the subject of my scholarship: modern Iran and the Iranian revolution. When he saw my puzzled face, he told me that he believed Western apprehension about Iran is actually rooted in apprehension about China. Arrighi thought that if there were a "mainstream" of world history, it ought to be located in the story of China, the only civilization

29 Giovanni Arrighi, *Adam Smith in Beijing: Lineages of the 21st Century*, London: Verso, 2009.

that has shaped the world as a hegemon over many millennia with the exception of the last 250 years. The rise of the West, according to him, is an aberration and China will define the future of world history. For China to play that role, it needs sources of energy to feed its expanding economy and a firm foothold in the world trade network. And there is Iran with its vast sources of oil and natural gas, located in a key strategic position guarding the flow of oil from the strait of Hormuz and offering open access to the Indian Ocean trade routes. I do not subscribe to the view that the US position on Iran can be reduced to a reflection of the American political establishment's attitude toward China. But there indeed are signs that Iran's east-bound realignment toward China is making possible a major transformation in the world political and economic order.

The fear in the West of a rising China became more acute this week with the announcement of a memorandum of understanding (MOU) between Iran and China of a 25-year trade agreement.[30] Although the text of the agreement has not been released, news outlets around the world were quick to sound the alarm of a pending major transformation of the balance of power in the Middle East and beyond. Many observers have seen the move as a direct consequence of the Trump administration's withdrawal from the Joint Comprehensive Plan of Action (JCPOA), also known as the Iran Nuclear Deal.

The Trump administration miscalculated the vulnerability of the Iranian government to his regime of maximum pressure. Trump

30 https://www.nytimes.com/2020/07/11/world/asia/china-iran-trade-military-deal.html

and his perpetually hawkish advisers believed that withdrawing from the nuclear deal, and re-imposing draconian sanctions against Iran, would compel the Islamic Republic either to surrender to the demands of its international foes, or to face the wrath of its own sullen citizens whose livelihoods the sanctions have directly threatened. The latter did materialize last November, but it was met with a swift and brutal reaction by the Iranian security forces.[31] The protests spread in many towns and cities around the country, but failed to sustain themselves in the face of the state's violent clampdown that left hundreds of protesters dead and thousands arrested.[32] According to the government's own estimate, 230 people were killed. In addition to the state repressive apparatus that contained the protests, Iranians also remain deeply inimical toward an American policy that invests in inflicting suffering on people in order to encourage them to rise up against their own government. Iranians are well-versed in this ploy, which offers a painful reminder of Saddam Hussein's justification of bombing Iranian cities. In order to stop the bombings, Hussein shamelessly declared, Iranians need to topple their regime.

The US pulled out of the JOCPA hoping that their withdrawal would render the agreement practically null and void. The Trump administration reinstituted crippling sanctions against Iran and exerted pressure on the EU and the UK to follow suit. Although

31 https://www.theguardian.com/commentisfree/2019/nov/26/the-guardian-view-on-irans-protests-unrest-is-crushed-unhappiness-endures

32 https://www.aljazeera.com/news/2019/12/17/vicious-crackdown-iran-protest-death-toll-at-304-amnesty-says/

the Europeans voiced their displeasure with the US policy, they could not deliver their share of the agreement under the mounting American pressures. This was a sobering moment for the Europeans as they witnessed the US's ability to impose its political will onto European banks and corporations. By threatening to levy sanctions against European banks and corporations that invest in the Iranian economy, in effect, the US undermined the sovereignty of the EU members over their own financial and economic affairs.

Whereas the Europeans saw in the US regime of maximum pressure against Iran the limits of their autonomy, China saw an opportunity for the realization of its global development strategy, known as the Belt and Road Initiative. The initiative that was adopted in 2013 envisions a massive expansion of trade networks by investing in infrastructures of land and sea transport that will eventually establish a seamless web of production, distribution, and consumption of goods: "a silk road for the twenty-first century," a phrase the Chinese used to promote the idea. Iran figures in this strategy mightily, both in terms of the extension of the *belt,* i.e. roads and railway, and *road,* i.e. the sea routes, as well as the source of energy that the Chinese expansionist machine requires. Today, China imports ten-million barrels of oil per day to fuel its economy.[33] Theoretically, Iran can provide half of that need for the next two decades. If China's plans to replace fossil fuel with the renewable energy do not pan out, Iran will remain a major source to calm the Communist Party's anxieties about the future of the silk road for the twenty-first century.

33 https://www.eia.gov/

The details of the trade agreement have not been released and both China and Iran still need to ratify it. The early reports indicate that China has agreed to a $400-billion investment over the next twenty-five years in the Iranian oil, gas, and transportation infrastructure. The investment will be frontloaded for the first five years and will also include cooperation in military and intelligence and a strategic alliance between the two countries over the security of the Persian Gulf trade routes. The agreement was first conceived during the Chinese Premier's visit to Iran in 2016. In all likelihood, it is going to end the Trump administration's gambit to cajole the Iranian side to capitulate and entertain a new nuclear treaty with the US and its Western allies.

The Iran-China agreement, if signed and ratified, will leave the Iranian exilic opposition, those who banked on the American maximum pressure on the Islamic Republic to gain political points, in an untenable position. These critics, who were also joined by the US State Department, have compared the proposed bilateral pact to the 1828 Treaty of Turkmenchay between Persia and Tsarist Russia, under which the Persians ceded control of the vast territories in the South Caucasus that included today's Armenia, Azerbaijan, Abkhazia, and Georgia. Ever since the mid-nineteenth century, in the Iranian political lexicon, "Turkmenchay" has remained a point of reference to the vilest encroachments on Iranian sovereignty. In the past two centuries, these encroachments have always been mounted by the same Western powers who forewarn Iranians today of the colonial consequences of surrendering the country's vast resources to the Chinese. No one knows whether this bilateral treaty would one-sidedly satisfy the Chinese imperial ambitions, a scenario that has played out in China's appropriation of African port cities and mining towns. But one thing is clear, that the objections of the US and their Iranian supporters, whatever those objections might be, do not stem from their concerns for the protection of the Iranian sovereignty and the Iranian people's interests.

13

Biden and Iran

February 2021

There is an expression in Persian that says "when an idiot throws a stone into a well, hundreds of wise people can't recover it." Now this is the story of Donald Trump's idiotic decision in May 2018 to withdraw from the 2015 nuclear agreement with Iran known as the Joint Comprehensive Plan of Action (JCPOA)[34] that the US had signed with China, France, Germany, the UK, and Russia. The agreement was also endorsed by the UN Security Council Resolution 2231.

The Trump administration's decision was in line with the Israeli and Saudi governments' position to derail the agreement. Both the Israelis and the Saudis vehemently opposed the JCPOA and

34 https://www.armscontrol.org/factsheets/joint-comprehensive-plan-action-jcpoa-glance

lobbied the White House aggressively to rescind its signature. Not only did the US withdraw, but the Trump administration also reinstated the sanctions against Iran and instituted an ever-expanding regime of maximum pressure tantamount to all-out economic warfare. By all accounts, the campaign of maximum pressure was a massive failure.[35] The American disavowal allowed Iran to limit its compliance with the deal and begin to incrementally violate the agreement. Additionally, the Trump administration's campaign of maximum pressure isolated the US internationally. This left it without recourse to exert any influence on its European allies to contain the Islamic Republic's gradual, but certain, path toward abandoning its commitments to the JCPOA.

During his campaign, Joe Biden never categorically declared that his administration would rejoin the Iran nuclear agreement. During the campaign, in a *CNN* op-ed, he wrote that he "will offer Tehran a credible path back to diplomacy. If Iran returns to strict compliance with the nuclear deal, the United States would rejoin the agreement as a starting point for follow-on negotiations."[36] Later, he continued that those negotiations would involve the Islamic Republic's violations of human rights and Iran's role in the regional conflicts. That convoluted position did not make it clear whether, as the President, Biden would return to the nuclear agreement without preconditions. This uncertainty became more evident. Unlike rejoining the

35 https://www.washingtonpost.com/world/2020/11/17/trump-iran-pressure-biden-nuclear/

36 https://www.cnn.com/2020/09/13/opinions/smarter-way-to-be-tough-on-iran-joe-biden/index.html

Paris Climate Accord and renewed membership in the World Health Organization with a prompt executive order, President Biden left the decision on reviving the JCPOA to an unspecified future date.

Last week's statements by the Biden appointees made the matter unnecessarily more complicated, sounding more like a continuation of the Trump policy rather than its refutation. In his confirmation hearing, Antony Blinken, Biden's choice for secretary of state, told the Senate Foreign Relations Committee that the new administration believes that Iran needs to resume strict compliance with the nuclear agreement before the US contemplates a return to the JCPOA. In response to the question of lifting the economic sanctions that the previous administration imposed on Iran, Blinken told the committee that "we are a long way from there." He further added, "We would then have to evaluate whether they were actually making good if they say they are coming back into compliance with their obligations, and then we would take it from there." The Biden administration's ultimate aim would be, he reiterated, a deal that also limited Iran's missile program and support for regional proxies.

In her confirmation testimony, Biden's pick for the director of national intelligence, Avril Haines, further complicated the formula on rejoining the nuclear agreement. "I think, frankly, we're long ways from that," she responded to Senator Susan Collins' inquiry. She then added that Biden and his team would "also have to look at the ballistic missile issues, as well as Iran's other 'destabilizing activities' before rejoining the nuclear agreement." And to leave no doubts, the White House Press Secretary Jen Psaki, made it abundantly clear that the president believes that "The United States should seek to lengthen and strengthen nuclear constraints on Iran and address other issues of concern. Iran must resume compliance with significant nuclear constraints under the deal in order for that to proceed."[37]

The Biden administration's demand that Iran must fulfill its obligations to an agreement from which the US has withdrawn is an Orwellian framing that was highlighted by the Iranian officials. In an op-ed in *Foreign Affairs*, Mohammad Javad Zarif, the Iranian Minister of Foreign Affairs, argued that the US needs to return to diplomacy and deliver its obligations to the document they signed in 2015. Once a party leaves an agreement, then that party has no authority demanding others' compliance with that agreement.[38] Zarif tweeted, "It was the US that broke the deal—for no reason. It must remedy its wrong; then Iran will respond."[39] The Iranian side argues that the US needs to rejoin the JCPOA and lift all the Trump-era sanctions without preconditions.

Although the appointment of Robert Malley as the special envoy for Iran sent a reconciliatory signal toward Iran, Antony Blinken, Malley's boss, remains unmoved. After taking office, Blinken reiterated his earlier position that the US will not return to the nuclear agreement before Iran's full compliance. On the first day of his new

37 https://www.vox.com/2021/1/19/22238707/haines-mayorkas-blinken-austin-confirmation-hearings-biden

38 https://www.foreignaffairs.com/articles/iran/2021-01-22/iran-wants-nuclear-deal-it-made

39 https://x.com/JZarif/status/1354089506861940736?ref_src=twsrc%5Etfw%7Ctwcamp%5Etweetembed%7Ctwterm%5E1354089506861940736%7Ctwgr%5E%7Ctwcon%5Es1_&ref_url=https%3A%2F%2Fwww.washingtonpost.com%2Fworld%2F2021%2F01%2F27%2Fbiden-iran-nuclear-deal-challenge%2F

role, Malley consulted the European partners to sketch a roadmap for reviving the agreement. On the same day, the French president threw another wrench into Malley's plans. President Emmanuel Macron stated that any "nuclear deal with Iran would be very strict and should include Saudi Arabia."[40] How Malley will navigate these terrains of competing interests, Saudi and Israeli pressures, and uncertain Biden policies remains to be seen.

Who goes first in returning to the nuclear agreement is the manifestation of a complex political problem. There is a very simple solution to the question of who goes first. No one. Both sides can very easily declare simultaneously that they are returning to the principles of the JCPOA. Both sides can set aside two weeks in order to offer proof of compliance. This is not a rocket science. But rocket science is exactly what is at stake for the US and its regional allies, the Gulf States, Saudi Arabia, and Israel. Significant pressures are mounting on the Biden administration to amend the nuclear deal to include containment of the Iranian missile program and the Islamic Republic's relations with its regional allies before reentering the deal. The Iranian side will not renegotiate the terms of the JCPOA, period.

There is another group of actors who see in Trump's withdrawal from the nuclear agreement an opportunity to pressure the Islamic Republic on its violations of human rights. A variety of Iranian opposition groups and expatriates argue that the US must include respect for human rights and civil liberties as a precondition for lifting the sanctions and normalized relations. It is a hard sell for those who are

---

40 https://www.reuters.com/article/france-iran-int/frances-macron-says-any-new-nuclear-talks-with-iran-to-be-strict-arabiya-tv-idUSKBN29Y2BT/

genuinely concerned with the question of human rights to ask the US government to be the agent of that change. So long as our government supports the region's most oppressive regimes, it is hard to imagine that it has any moral authority or political capital to spend on issues of human rights in Iran. It is deeply cynical to suggest the US government as an advocate of human rights and civil liberties in Iran while it continues to support regimes in whose prisons and occupied lands millions of people are languishing in despair.

There are innumerable problems in Iran, political repression, economic despair, social discontent, gender-ethnic-religious discriminations, deep economic corruption, and crony capitalism. But the US cannot and should not be the agent of change in Iran. I do not know how many times in history that simple fact has been proven. There is in Iran a vibrant society that engages these problems at so many different levels. These engagements have brought about significant changes in the country and its political establishment and continue to do so. The best way for Americans to support these transformations is to stop the sanctions and stay clear of the Iranian domestic affairs.

US sanctions and policies of different administrations toward Iran have not produced results that will benefit Iranian people. In Iran:

- Sanctions have deepened the securitization of society
- Sanctions have weakened civil society
- Sanctions have created informal economies that lack transparency
- Sanctions have increased corruption and has entrenched crony capitalism
- Sanctions have given rise to bellicose politics

- Sanctions have deepened pauperization of the masses
- Sanctions have inflicted unwarranted pain on ordinary people

More than thirty years ago, Henry Precht, then the head of the Iran desk at the State Department, offered an astute observation that unfortunately still holds true. "The American consensus on Iran is persistent and clear," he wrote in 1988. "The leaders in Tehran are crazy, blindly ideological, resistant to international law and opinion, and virtually impossible to deal with. And the bad news only gets worse from this wild bunch." He argued that what motivates the Islamic Republic is "political and economic independence at home, not dominion abroad."[41] That is why I believe that the solution to the crisis in Iran-US relations was already devised forty years ago in Algiers. In the accord that was signed in 1981, the US pledged that "it is now and will be the policy of the US not to intervene, directly or indirectly, politically or militarily, in Iran's internal affairs."[42]

Successive American governments have tried and failed to come to terms with the sovereignty of the Iranian government. A pledge of non-interference and demonstrating that pledge in practice will be the most remarkable gift that the Biden administration can offer Iranian people. By perpetuating a foreign threat, the Biden administration would only stifle demands for social change and political reform from inside the country by those who are persistently exercising their right to self-determination.

---

41 Henry Precht, "Ayatollah Realpolitik," *Foreign Policy,* no. 70 (Spring, 1988), pp, 109-128.

42 https://www.parstimes.com/history/algiers_accords.pdf, p. 1.

SECTION III

AMERICAN POLITICS

American domestic politics is invariably informed by the logic of empire. What happens in the US has far-reaching consequences around the world. By and large, Republicans and Democrats share a common vision about the global role of the US. With the election of Barack Obama, there were hopes that his presidency would set a different kind of precedent in the American political project. Domestically and internationally, the promise of change and hope never materialized. The essays in this section engage with the unremitting shift to the right in American politics—a shift that has transformed the political landscape of the US domestically and internationally, while at the same time has been met with significant resistance.

14
Obama and the Iron Cage

November 2008

Can Barack Obama transcend the Iron Cage of the White House? The short answer to the question is a simple no!

I hoped with all my might that Obama would win the presidency and end the reign of terror that the Bush Administration has inflicted on the world. Much more needs to be said about the historical significance of a White House with Black residents, but not here. I am jubilant that he has won and apprehensive about how soon he and his administration will capitulate to the habitual politics of DC. Obama has the power to resist the current, but he won't. To do that, he would have to launch a paradigmatic shift in the way politics is taught, thought of, and practiced in this country.

Obama ran a presidential campaign with an inherent contradiction between its form and substance. In its form—the ways his campaign mobilized different constituencies, the way he appeared in rallies, and in the very intonation of his oratory—he presented himself as a populist candidate advocating radical change. Substantively—in his economic plan, in his understanding of global conflicts, and in his political vision—he differentiated himself by a hair's breadth from Clinton-era center-right doctrine. History tells us that substance is enduring and form is ephemeral.

In the US, the real polity consists of a small community of elites whose interests and those they represent entangle and overlap. President-elect Obama, with all good intentions, intends to erect a wall between lobbyists and elected or appointed officials, but he will soon realize that the foundation that could support such a wall does not exist. DC operatives, the political elite, and corporate lobbyists have been engaged in an incestuous relation for too long for any sense of taboo to remain in force, even weakly. No one is stunned these days at the sight of a CEO of a financial giant being named as the chief regulator of the nation's stock market. No one questions the lobbyists of multinational industries running the office of the Environmental Protection Agency. No eyebrows would be raised if yesterday's corporate lawyer is today's Secretary of Labor. No one detects a conflict of interest if big military contractors devise a national security plan at the Pentagon and the State Department. In the way politics actually gets done in Washington, can Obama find people who meet his criteria without stepping outside the conventional norms of the American political machine? I'm skeptical.

Obama also needs to learn a lesson from the leaders of populist movements, particularly in Latin America. I am not a fan of populism. It thrives on creating a mass society, which in turn, typically engenders authoritarianism. In the last four decades, populism has always been associated with the American Right, religious and otherwise. This association has caused many of us to connect populism unconsciously to simple-mindedness and gullibility. The McCain-Palin campaign adopted this Right-wing populism rather successfully in mocking Obama's plan to "spread the wealth" through a "socialist" agenda. Whereas protecting the "authentic" American community from the tyranny of the interventionist state defines the right-wing populism, the cause célèbre of left-wing populism has been "redistributive justice," often associated with socialism. To be true to his constituents, Obama must defuse the socialist associations of the old slogan and transform the notion of redistributive justice from being a near-treasonous heresy to a viable policy direction for the US.

The scarecrow of socialism lost its political appeal in Europe almost a century ago. But it continues to stifle meaningful debate about the foundational problems of the American economic order. Latin American populist leaders on the left understand—in a way that American politicians don't—that people respond to their genuine fears (cultural, communal, familial, etc.) as well as their core economic interests. Which one will dominate on Election Day depends on which political discourse becomes hegemonic. The masses are neither inherently right nor historically left. This was an important oversight in Obama's campaign. The precondition of rallying the masses and becoming hegemonic is not a move to the center-right, but a strategy to use language to dominate politics, to introduce not only new faces, but also new concepts to US politics. A strategy that Republicans have deployed successfully for decades.

For the longest time during the past year, when Obama was "accused" of being a Muslim, I wondered why nobody in his campaign stood up and said what eventually Colin Powell said in his endorsement: "What if he is? Is there something wrong with being a Muslim in this country? The answer's no, that's not America." Obama needs an appointed person to do with social democracy what Powell did to Muslims. He needs to appoint somebody with enough audacity and hope in his administration to transform redistributive justice from political suicide into a debatable agenda. Even with his centrist agenda, this will be good for his administration.

The time is right for such a discursive and political move. The election is over, and Obama does not need to blame only the Bush Administration for all the ills of deregulationism. This policy began in the mid-1970s, found its official voice in the Reagan Administration, and has been followed since by Democrats and Republicans alike. And let us not forget that the economic team that the President-elect has put together looks a lot like the deregulation team of Bill Clinton. Obama is making a historical mistake. His hope should not be to bring back the Clinton regime back minus Lewinsky. If we all agree that the scope of this economic crisis is comparable to the Great Depression, then we cannot simply write off extraordinary social provisions as politically untenable.

This is turning into a vicious pattern, that at points of crises all parties scoff at long-term solutions in favor of quick fixes. If we are in Iraq, we don't need to talk about the political responsibilities for this travesty: we need to fix the problem now. If the stock market has collapsed: rush for a bailout, and address reform later. These kinds of solutions perpetuate injustice and inequality, and negate accountability and the feasibility of new visions. We need immediate remedies tied with written and sealed regulatory guarantees. The banking bailout should have come with stern restrictions on financial and industrial capital. Remember that the collapse of the economy has universal repercussions. If the economic elite uses the threat of economic collapse to get what they desire, shouldn't Obama's administration of hope and change ask for the same on behalf of the disadvantaged? President Obama should not retreat from higher taxes and tighter regulations on the industry. In times of prosperity, investors exploit the mobility of their capital to avoid regulatory regimes. Today, they do not have that luxury.

On national security and the so-called Global War on Terror, Obama needs to take a radical discursive shift. Does he have the power to do it? Yes. Will he? No. The main objective of a sound international relations is the discovery of the ways through which the US can reconcile its national interests with the national interests of other nations. The Cold War mentality of irreconcilable American interests with other nations has already taken millions of lives around the world, during the proxy wars in Africa, Asia, and Latin America to stop the spread of communism, and now in the "war on terror" to eradicate militant Islam.

Obama must take advantage of the excitement and energy that enveloped the entire world, from the celebrations in an Indonesian grade school to the ritual sacrifices of lamb in his honor in Istanbul, to show in practice that the era of American bullying is over and his administration is ready to engage the world with mutual respect. But before we gloat out of our minds and ask the rest of the world that instead of celebrating "show us the money," as Thomas Friedman suggested in his Sunday editorial, Obama needs to deliver. Unlike what the likes of Friedman would like to think, the world is not indebted to the US, it is really, truly, the other way around. Respect for the dignity of others and the sovereignty of nations is not delivered in a speech. Obama, as the President, needs to institutionalize that rhetoric and turn it into a lasting policy. "The money" would follow. Friedman don't rush, the world cannot afford to give a blank check to any American president, be it the decent Obama or the gangster Bush.

Obama knows that the key to a sustainable peaceful coexistence in the world today is held in the Middle East. Again, the first signs are not promising. In his official Afghanistan policy, which was rightly described by John McCain as a replica of the surge in Iraq, Obama has shown little understanding of the political dynamics of the conflict. His solutions appear to be variations on the same "war on terror" theme. The US cannot defeat the Taliban and annihilate al-Qaeda by introducing more troops to the war front. Obama must take the option of war off the table; nothing terrible would happen if he takes this courageous step. Not only would taking war off the table afford the respect that the US desires in the region, but more importantly it will instantly delegitimize the militants' violent solutions. There is no shame in talking, there is shame in sending innocent people to their death.

This must also be the guiding principle in dealing with Iran. The US has no right or responsibility to solve Iranian domestic problems. Obama should stay clear from the Israeli lobby on dealing with Iran. Although that option might already have been checked by the appointment of Rahm Immanuel, a hawkish pro-Israel advocate, as the Chief of Staff and choosing Dennis Ross as a senior advisor on the Middle East policy. Since September 11, 2001, the neocons have successfully manufactured a crisis with Iran based on unfounded allegations and regime change policies. It is true that the Bush Administration pulled the rug from under the Iranian reformist President Khatami's feet and paved the way for the inauguration of an equally hostile administration in Iran. President Obama need not buy into this manufactured crisis. Iran's nuclear technology is not an irresolvable predicament. While solving the problem with Iran might ease the situation in Iraq, it is doubtful that it would have any impact on the Israeli-Palestinian conflict. The Iranian influence in Palestine is greatly exaggerated. This too is another part of America's fabricated crisis in Iran.

As hard as it might be, the Obama administration must face the possibility of decoupling its interest in the Middle East from the Israelis. One can hope. The US cannot operate as a peace broker while it unconditionally supports Israeli policies. There are more critical voices inside Israel on their own state policies than in any American administration or mass media. Being critical of Israeli settlement policies and the illegal occupation of Palestinian territories will neither endanger Israeli security and its right to exist, nor is it a sign of anti-Semitism. No US state official has more credibility in the Middle East than former President Jimmy Carter. Carter broke another taboo in American foreign policy by talking to Hamas leaders and by doing so, proved that he indeed had the audacity to hope for peace. Obama must immediately dispatch a committee under the supervision of Carter to lay out a plan for a lasting peace agreement between Israel and Palestine.

My hope is that an Obama administration would augment the spark of November 4th into a flame that will guide us on a path towards sustainable change. We dared to hope. Obama must now have the courage to deliver. There are many taboos in American political culture that he must break. Many call people who talk about social democracy, peace, justice, equality, and respect for the dignity of others "crazies." But this is a crazy time, a Black man rules over the White House.

15

Bombs in Gaza Wound Academic Freedom in Urbana-Champaign

September 2014

I write as a professor of History and Sociology at the University of Illinois, Urbana-Champaign. I have long taken pride in the University of Illinois as a highly respected public university in the country, as a place in which Nobel Prize winners work, pathbreaking early computers were built, award-winning research is conducted, and world-class scholars teach and sustain a highly vibrant world of ideas. I used to see the name of my institution in light of these significant grounds. Not anymore.

I write also to appeal to all those who care about and appreciate the significance of academic freedom because they understand how this precious value contributes to the well-being of our society. I hope that by reading this you will feel as outraged and troubled as many of us at the University of Illinois feel. This is not a highbrow predicament of the intellectual elite. This is a crisis of one of the most important foundations of our increasingly deteriorating democracy, that of freedom of expression and the right to have an institutional voice against the corporatization of American universities.

I recently came back from Jakarta, where I was participating in a scholarly conference. On several occasions during my short trip, my Indonesian colleagues asked me whether I was from the same institution that "fired" that English professor. I was shocked by how fast the embarrassing news of our administration's misconduct travelled half the world and turned an institution to which many of us proudly belong, into the subject of the most depressing academic news cycles.

Alas, this is not the case these days. From a piece in *Haaretz*[43] to an editorial in *Inside Higher Education*,[44] from the Illinois AAUP[45] committee to a whole host of bloggers from across the country, academics have denounced the Chancellor of University of Illinois' decision to rescind the hiring of Professor Steven Salaita for his incendiary tweets against the Israeli attacks on civilians in Gaza. Chancellor Wise has reportedly informed Salaita that the university has voided a job offer that was extended to him earlier this past year. The news came nearly ten months after Salaita had signed an offer letter, at a time when he had already resigned from his position as an Associate

43 https://www.haaretz.com/jewish/2014-08-06/ty-article/u-s-professor-loses-job-over-anti-israel-tweets/0000017f-e545-d62c-a1ff-fd7fafb50000

44 Scott Jaschik, "Out of a Job," *Inside Higher Education*, August 5, 2014.

45 https://academeblog.org/2014/08/06/illinois-aaup-committee-a-statement-on-steven-salaita-and-uiuc/

Professor of English at Virginia Tech with the understanding that he was to move to Urbana-Champaign with his family. His courses were already enrolled, and he was to begin teaching in a few weeks.

It is also now revealed that Wise made her decision in response to outside pressures. The university responded to an open records request from *Inside Higher Education* for communications to the chancellor about the Salaita appointment, prior to her action to block it.[46] The communications show that Wise was lobbied on the decision not only by pro-Israel students, parents, and alumni, but also by the fundraising arm of the university. The communications also show that the university system president was involved, and that the university was considering the legal ramifications of the case before the action to block the appointment. According to *Haaretz*, the Simon Wiesenthal Center sent a letter to Robert Easter, President of the University of Illinois, protesting the appointment of Salaita. The letter characterizes Salaita as a "misguided academic" who "spews venomous and mendacious analogies" about Israel and raises the question: "What possible prestige can Salaita add to the UI faculty?" An op-ed piece in Urbana-Champaign local newspaper, *The News Gazette*, also published a series of decontextualized inflammatory posts from Salaita's personal Twitter account (see Phan Nguyen for the context of the tweets[47]) and echoed other conservative lobbyists in calling on the University's Board of Trustees to block his appointment.

---

46 Scott Jaschik, "The Emails on Salaita," *Inside Higher Ed*, August 24, 2014.

47 https://mondoweiss.net/2014/08/reading-salaita-illinois-1/#tweet1

More than 16,000 people have already signed a Petition asking Wise to reconsider her decision and to reinstate Salaita's appointment.[48] In a strong statement, the American Association of University Professors argued on behalf of Salaita and that his and the faculty of the University of Illinois' academic freedom has been violated. More than 3,000 scholars have so far boycotted the University of Illinois, cancelling lectures, refusing to write letters of recommendation or participate in peer review.

Wise claims that by her decision she was merely protecting the dignity and interests of students whose sensibilities Salaita disregarded by his inflammatory tweets. Had she consulted with the search committee and others who carefully vetted his dossier, she would have known that Salaita's teaching record is exemplary by any standard. The record shows that his pedagogical approach and his classroom presence has by no means been compromised by his political commitments and ethical imperatives which motivate his public engagement with the Israeli-Palestinian conflict. The teaching record in his file shows that in the category of "concern and respect" for students, according to documents posted on *Mondoweiss,* "Salaita has earned an incredibly high evaluation from the students in the last six courses he taught in his former institution. Here is where students evaluate their professor for professional empathy, respect for diverse points of view, and sensitivity to student opinion and student lives."[49]

---

48 https://www.change.org/p/reinstate-professor-steven-salaita

49 https://mondoweiss.net/2014/08/teaching-political-motivation/

Here is a sample from Professor Salaita's official teaching evaluation:

> *30 Total: 28 Excellent, 2 Good*
> *30 Total: 30 out of 30 Excellent*
> *10 Total: 10 out of 10 Excellent*
> *29 Total: 28 Excellent, 1 Good*
> *28 Total: 28 out of 28 excellent*

The Salaita affair has exposed a larger trend in the corporatization of American universities. Many of us might disagree with Salaita's comments and the tone in which he delivered them. But the general public, as well as university presidents, need to be concerned about the ominous precedent that is being set by the Chancellor and the Board of Trustees at the University of Illinois. What makes American institutions of higher education distinct, intellectually vibrant, and academically rich lies exactly in the principle of the separation of scholarly affairs from business and political considerations.

Universities have always struggled for inclusion, for diversity (of ideas and people), for deeper thinking and wider outreach. It has always been the faculty and students who have pushed for change against the resistance of a variety of higher education administrations. It has always been the faculty and students who pushed to hire women, to hire African Americans, to hire other minorities, to hire Jews without prejudice, to defy the stigma associated with sexual preferences, to include and give significance to ethnic studies, to protect unpopular and controversial ideas. There is not a single case that any of these changes were instituted top-down by any university administration, no matter how progressive and open-minded they were. There is a long history that emerging ideas and the outspoken advocates of those ideas were characterized as "uncivil," "subversive," or "incendiary." It is unfortunate that Wise and her supporters have yet again introduced "civility," a worn-out, racially charged, and gendered device of exclusion in justifying the decision to void Salaita's appointment.

All of that could be done precisely because universities operate based on the principle of shared governance. Shared governance checks the Administration's authority over substantive issues of merit and scholarship and protects the independence of academic units and departments. This is where the difference lies between a university and a corporation. The Chancellor of a university cannot and should not exercise the authority of her office in the same vein as the CEO of a company. Shared governance means that she must abide by and respect faculty deliberations and decisions regarding academic matters. The determination of what is acceptable discourse and how it furthers or hinders discussion in a field is not the responsibility of the Chancellor or the Board of Trustees. These are offices that are readily susceptible to and swayed by outside political pressures and donors' proclivities. As the Salaita affair demonstrates.

By rescinding Salaita's appointment, in effect, Wise has turned a pro forma step in the process of hiring new faculty (and potentially in faculty promotion) into an active vetting procedure. Such scrutiny at the managerial level inevitably undermines the integrity and autonomy of faculty governance. This is a serious issue for all university campuses to confront with diligence and care. Under the existing order, the administration shares and communicates any grave concerns about new hires or promotions with the relevant departments or units. If the new order persists and spreads to other campuses around the country, it will inevitably transfer authority and discretion away from faculty and endow the already growing class of administrative managers with unprecedented oversight and veto power. In addition to its political context, as Timothy Burke eloquently argues, the Salaita Affair is about restructuring university governance and facilitating the migration of practical authority and decision-making upwards.[50]

There are two precedents being set at Illinois: One by the administration and the other by the faculty and students. The former will make the universities increasingly vulnerable to the demands of private donors and political ambitions of its administration. The latter intends to uphold hard fought and earned rights of free expression, academic freedom, and the institutional autonomy of scholarly inquiry. Let us hope that the latter wins. Universities must be defended! Please do your share!

---

50 https://blogs.swarthmore.edu/burke/blog/2014/08/22/on-the-salaita-decision/index.html

16
Biden and the Commonsense Voter

June 2020

Last Friday, on the *PBS News Hour's* weekly review with Mark Shields and David Brooks, Judy Woodruff posed a question about Joe Biden's response to what was happening in Minneapolis. Brooks, the *New York Times'* conservative columnist, visibly shaken by the events of the week, declared: "I want to see more outrage. I want to see outrage at a president who's grown more contemptible by the day, including his tweets about what happened in Minneapolis. I want to see somebody addressing the underlying issues that lead to the inequalities in places like Minneapolis and all around the country. I just want to see a more aggressive Democratic challenger, who's really got broad arguments for collective change, structural change. I want to see a candidate who is as angry as he ought to be, to be honest."

As I sat there watching this episode, I wondered if we have reached a point where Biden's prosaic comments, and the incoherence with which he delivers them, perturbs a conservative columnist, what should such banality do to the progressives of this land?[51] When Brooks talks about "collective and structural change," what kind of responsibilities does that generate for those of us who have inherited that desire from successive generations who have been demanding those changes since the beginning of the so-called "American experiment?"

The time has come to end this crooked charade of electoral politics that has perpetuated the hegemony of a corrupt two-party system and think about the real possibilities of a radical democracy—a democratic system that is built on the foundations of social justice. The vicious circle of voting for the Democrats' candidate, no matter how corrupt the party and its nominees are, needs to end. We are always told that *the time is not right.* Yet, we never hear what the right time would be and when it would arrive. Under what circumstances does one vote her conscience?

If there were any doubts that the powers that be would not allow the realization of any meaningful choice in the presidential elections, those doubts should have been put to rest after the Clinton-DNC staged a coup against Bernie Sanders during the last presidential campaign. Any genuine examination of how Donald Trump ended up in the White House, must have interrogated the DNC conspiracy to sabotage Sanders' campaign rather than the wild goose

51 https://www.pbs.org/newshour/show/biden-george-floyds-death-is-no-time-for-incendiary-tweets

chase of the Russian interference, true as it might have been. The DNC handed the presidency to Trump. And they will end up doing it again.

The early success of Sanders' campaign in 2020 alarmed the party again and made its leadership visibly concerned about the possibility of a contested nomination process. President Obama came out of his long silence since he had left office to assure the party leadership that he would speak up to stop Bernie Sanders' nomination.[52] Through a combination of the old party patronage system, disenfranchisement, fear mongering, and campaigns of misinformation, the DNC pulled Biden from the bottom of the list and crowned him at the top as the "presumptive" nominee. A man who could not articulate a thought without meandering sentences and bouts of forgetfulness that alarmed many observers about his mental fitness, became the one who is now to rescue the country from the rising tide of fascism.

The same party leadership that utterly failed to understand that the fault lines of the last presidential election were a vote for or against the establishment and rallied behind Hillary Clinton, who epitomized all that is wrong with the existing order, is now counting on the loyalty of the hardcore Democrats to take back the White House with Biden. I am not here to say that Biden cannot win. He might. Trump might have alienated enough people with his vulgarity, diseased mind, nefarious heart, and devious personality that would

52 https://www.huffpost.com/entry/obama-bernie-sanders-2020-nomination_n_5ddd31a1e4b00149f724793b

cost him the presidency. But that cannot vindicate the misdeeds of the DNC and absolve the corruption at its heart.

The Left cannot afford and should not give another pass to the DNC oligarchy. The party has shown time and again that it is incapable of foundational transformation. What people on the streets of Minneapolis, Houston, Los Angeles, New York City, Chicago, Atlanta, and many other major cities in the country are crying out for is not to bring to the office a kinder, gentler, corrupt politician who opposed the necessity of "collective and structural changes" in American society. The Left has given enough carte blanche to the Democrats, the time has come for real accountability.

Biden is corrupt. Not once during the entire House investigation of Trump's abuse of power in looking into Hunter Biden's lucrative seat on the board of Burisma, a Ukrainian energy company, were any Democrat eyebrows raised about what actually he, the son of the then Vice President of the United States, was doing on that board making hundreds of thousands of dollars a year for doing absolutely nothing. Yes, Trump abused the power of his office and asked foreign entities to abet his presidential campaign. But that does not exonerate Biden. Is there any doubt in any one's mind that Hunter was sitting on that board because he was Biden's son? The time for bringing back the old corrupt machine is over.

I know that many people believe that the next presidential election is about ending Trump's presidency by all votes necessary. Biden only stands as non-Trump and for that he deserves our vote. From pragmatic and ethical standpoints, this position is problematic.

Pragmatically, Biden is perhaps the least electable candidate who could run against Trump. Trump and his advisors did their best to assure that Biden would win the nomination, he was the weak link in that crowded pack of nominees. He, similar to Hillary Clinton, is vulnerable to charges of corruption and representing the old corrupt machine. He is the candidate of business-as-usual. Again, I think he might even win on that kind of ticket, but I do not think in that case he wins the election, rather, it means that Trump loses it. Also, in his earlier years, Biden gained the infamy of making off-the-cuff comments about things that he later regretted or turned out to be lies. Indeed, that was always one of the reasons that he had to drop out of the party's nomination races. Today, he lacks spontaneity and struggles to maintain a clear head in debates and conversations. Trump has banked on this. He will have a sizeable return on that investment.

Ethically, the Left will not be responsible for a Trump second term. If Biden loses, all responsibility goes back to the party leadership and those oligarchical networks that work to undermine and sabotage the possibilities of real changes in American political order and economic system. It is abundantly clear that even if Biden wins, the Left and progressives will be kicking this can down the road, the can that has been opened and its fascist worms with their poisonous venom are crawling out of it. A Biden presidency will allow this mode of resentment against the system to grow in popularity and return with a more vengeful force that can then be more easily appropriated by supremacist, misogynist, and xenophobic forces. So, even if Biden loses, the progressives still can win. The Left needs to offer and rally around alternatives that will attract the downtrodden and the disenfranchised. Trump is not the end of the rise of fascism, it is its beginning. The more the progressives align themselves with candidates and alternatives of the establishment, the greater the space for the fascists to mobilize the disenfranchised.

The progressives need to assert themselves and force Biden's campaign to accommodate, in a meaningful way, their demands and run on a structurally transformative platform. Otherwise, a vote for Biden is a vote against the principles of democratic participation. Vote your conscience!

17
The Two-Headed Hydra of Racism and Imperialism

June 2020

Black Lives Matter (BLM) has raised mass consciousness against the institution of police violence and the brutality it inflicts on Black communities around the country. The movement has placed the question of police brutality at the top of the political and juridical reform agenda. The naked display of the oppressive state apparatus has now forced everyone, from the fascist residents of the White House to the liberal democrats of the House, politicians speak of the need to reform policing—more training, more screening, more record-keeping, judicial vigilance, and other haphazard sutures for the centuries-old wounds. Many observers have pointed out the depth of this chronic pain[53] and different ways it might be remedied.[54]

Here I would like to propose that this acutely American dilemma needs to be viewed and explicated in close relation to US colonialism and imperialism. Race relations in the US and the violence with which the country operates has always been accompanied by the civilizing logic of colonial expansion and imperialist wars that the US has raged around the world. The two heads of the hydra of imperialism and racism stem from the same body of the political order that defined this imperialized nation from its inception. So long as the American war machine runs on high gear, leaving destruction, devastation, and death around the world, here at home, Black Americans will not be treated as equal citizens. Drone attacks overseas are inherently linked to the murderous impulse of the police against Black Americans.

The concomitant rise of liberal political philosophy and modern colonialism is an established historical fact. One might still question whether colonialism and the atrocities through which it expanded ought to be regarded as an aberration in liberal thought or as an inherent feature of its worldview. But one thing is clear, the British and American founding fathers of liberalism did not understand democracy and colonialism in mutually exclusive terms, both were understood to be different elements of the same civilizing project. Far from contradicting liberal tenets, writes Uday Mehta, imperialism

---

53 Keeanga-Yamahtta Taylor, "How Do We Change America," *The New Yorker*, June 8, 2020. https://www.newyorker.com/news/our-columnists/how-do-we-change-america

54 William Barber II, Liz Theoharis, Timothy B. Tyson and Cornel West, "What the Courage to Change History Looks Like," *New York Times*, June 19, 2020.

in fact stemmed from liberal assumptions about reason and historical progress.[55] Evoking the same sentiment, more than a century ago, Jamal al-Afghani (1838-1897), the anti-colonial Muslim transnationalist, ridiculed the seemingly incongruous attitude of British colonialists in India: "They drew their swords to cut the throats of the Muslims, while weeping for them and crying: 'We kill you only out of compassion and pity for you, and seeking to improve you and make your life comfortable.'"[56]

No other liberal philosopher has articulated and justified this contradiction better than John Stuart Mill. His philosophy made clear the entanglement of liberal political thought with colonial expansion. Mill, like his father James, was an employee of the British East India Company. But economic interest alone cannot explain his ideological commitment to the idea of progress and the higher civilization that the British afforded the backward Indians. He believed that the transmission of civilization to colonized subjects could only materialize through a benevolent despotism. "England," Mill believed, "had a right to rule despotically because it brought the benefits of higher civilization." In a chilling assertion in his *Principles of Political Economy,* Mill declared that "the question of government intervention in the work of Colonization involves the future and permanent interests of civilization itself."[57]

55 Uday Singh Mehta, *Liberalism and Empire: A Study in Nineteenth-Century British Liberal Thought,* Chicago: University of Chicago Press, 1999.

56 Al-Afghani, "The Materialists in India," in N. Keddie, *An Islamic Response to Imperialism,* Berkeley: University of California Press, 1968, p. 179.

57 Cited in Eileen P. Sullivan, "Liberalism and Imperialism: J. S. Mill's Defense of the British Empire," *Journal of the History of Ideas,* vol. 44, no. 4 (October-December 1983), pp. 599-617.

There is no doubt that the plunder of human and natural resources of the colonies shaped imperial expansions. But the reality that the inhabitants of Africa, Asia, Oceania, and South America were all subjected to these atrocities has roots in a racialized worldview that gave legitimacy to Europeans to situate themselves on top of the racial hierarchy as the torch bearers of reason and progress. The light of the world was the Europeans' gift to all nations to overcome their superstitions, ignorance, tyranny, and backwardness. The light was lit by prey and pray, by plunder and proselytizing, by power and pauperization, and by pots and pans.

THE LIGHT OF THE WORLD.

"FRANK" RIPPINGILLE'S
ENGLAND'S GIFT
A BLESSING TO ALL NATIONS
FRANK RIPPINGILLE STOVE Co.
SOLE & ORIGINAL MANUFACTURERS OF THE
WORLD RENOWNED OIL COOKING STOVES
Works, PLUME
ASTON
BIRMINGHAM
PATENT
COOKING
STOVES

Despite her own prejudicial views on race, in *The Origins of Totalitarianism,* Hannah Arendt highlights that it was European imperialists who initially reordered mankind into master and slave races, into higher and lower breeds, into colored peoples and white men during their conquest and exploitation of much of Asia, Africa, and America. That is how the ruling classes "imperialized the nation," by expanding and acquiring new territories abroad and by solidifying and policing racial hierarchies at home. Expressed in no ambiguous terms by Woodrow Wilson, the US president during the Great War, the goal was clear, to keep the white race strong and to preserve white civilization and its domination of the planet.[58]

The eugenicist structure of white supremacy that motivated great European and American ruling classes operated with great consistency within and outside national boundaries. The same generals who led the American conquest of the Philippines in 1898-1902 fought the wars of annihilation against American Indians at home. One of them, Brigadier General Jacob H. Smith, explicitly stated in his order to the troops that "I want no prisoners. I wish you to kill and burn. The more you kill and burn, the better it will please me." More than 200,000 civilians were massacred during the war. During a Senate hearing on the atrocities in the Philippines, General Arthur MacArthur (father of Douglas) referred to the "magnificent Aryan peoples" he belonged to and the "unity of the race" he felt compelled to uphold.[59]

58 Hannah Arendt, *The Origins of Totalitarianism,* Cleveland and New York: Meridian Books, 1962.

59 Pankaj Mishra, "How the Colonial violence Came Home: The Ugly Truth of the First World War," *The Guardian,* Friday, November 10, 2017.

At the end of both world wars, sustaining the purity of whiteness and racial boundaries became increasingly challenging. The world wars shook the old structure of colonialism to its core. But that did nothing to change the colonial powers' perception of racial superiority. Learning from the experiences of the two wars, the emerging superpowers, the US and the Soviet Union, entered a "Cold War" that meant that superpowers ought not to fight their wars in the European theater. Cold War was a misnomer. Proxy wars raged around the world and claimed more than twenty million lives from 1946 to 1989. The old colonial structures had collapsed, but the propagated racialized ideology that peoples of Asia, Africa, Latin, and Central America were incapable of exercising the right of self-determination persisted.

As the atrocities of American superpower proliferated around the world, Black Americans struggled for recognition of political rights and social justice at home. Despite legal gains, the ideology that incentivized the US to commit mass murder around the globe, disincentivized it to put in place meaningful structural changes that would recognize racial hierarchies that informed the existing political order. The growing Black population in Europe, Afro-Caribbean, North African, and South Asians among others, forced European states to face the consequences of their colonial past on the streets of Paris, Berlin, Amsterdam, and London. What the authors of *The Empire Strikes Back* wrote almost forty years ago about the UK eerily resonates today with Trump's America "the construction of an authoritarian state in Britain is fundamentally intertwined with the elaboration of popular racism." The kind of racism that has historically been exercised through colonialism, slavery, segregation, ghettoization, militarized border controls, and mass incarceration.[60]

Racism was and is not about an attitude. Rather, it is the problem of a political order that sustains and perpetuates that attitude through a complex system of legal and economic institutions at home and around the world. Black Lives Matter protests have now razed or forced the local and federal agencies to remove monuments that celebrated the legacies of slavery, lynching, and segregation. Corporate America now "recognizes" the pandemic of racism.[61] Nike employees were offered a paid holiday on Juneteenth. The same goes for workers at Twitter, Target, General Motors, the National Football League, and a variety of other businesses. JPMorgan, Chase, Capital One and other banks will close branches early. All those institutions that maintain and perpetuate the dominance of racism and imperialism are at work to coopt the movement. Centuries of racism in the US will not wane by bringing down statues or tearing down monuments, despite their significant symbolic values, or having a half-day off at JPMorgan. The entire American political order, economic organization, and social hierarchies are informed by the question of race and a commitment to white supremacy. The veneer of great American ideology of meritocracy and opportunity is crumbling. The US needs that ideology, the "American dream," a myth that turned the land of slavery and indigenous annihilation

---

60 Center for Contemporary Cultural Studies, *Empire Strikes Back: Race and Racism in 70's Britain,* London, Routledge, 1982.

61 Gillian Friedman, "Here's What Companies are Promising to Do to Fight Racism," *New York Times,* August 23, 2020.

into the land of milk and honey. "This mythology is not benign," as Keeanga-Yamahtta Taylor explores, "it serves as the United States' self-declared invitation to intervene militarily and economically around the globe." The US needs to conceal its racial injustices at home in order to advance and legitimize its imperialist ambitions around the globe.[62]

Police brutality is inextricably linked to the military-industrial complex. This link is not only through the sales of surplus hardware, uniforms, and other equipment. Yes, the military leadership stood firm against Trump's recent transgressions and reminded him that the military cannot get involved in suppressing the right of protest for US citizens.[63] But since its inception, the same military has operated as the instrument of imperialist projects that carried out mass murders and subjugated people of color around the world. In his recent book, *Jakarta Method: Washington's anti-Communist Crusade & the Mass Murder Program That Shaped Our World,* Vincent Bivens shows how the US masterminded the project of annihilation of communists and members of labor unions in Indonesia during the 1965 coup against the nationalist leader Sukarno.[64] Although all the documents about the CIA involvement in the coup that brought the tyrannical regime of Suharto to power are not yet released,

---

62 Keeanga-Yamahtta Taylor, *From #BlackLivesMatter to Black Liberation,* Chicago: Haymarket Books, 2016.

63 https://www.aljazeera.com/news/2020/6/4/revolt-of-the-generals-trump-faces-heat-from-us-military-leaders

64 Vincent Bevins, *The Jakarta Method: Washington's Anticommunist Crusade and the Mass Murder Program that Shaped Our World,* New York: PublicAffairs Books, 2020.

those declassified documents published by the National Security Archive show how CIA operatives provided the names of unionists and members of Indonesian Communist Party to death squads for extermination.[65] According to more conservative estimates between 500,000 to one million people were massacred during the coup. More than one million were sent to concentration camps, many of whom vanished. Later it became evident, as Bivens discloses, that it wasn't only US government officials who handed over kill lists to the Army. Managers of US-owned plantations furnished them with the names of "troublesome" communists and union organizers, who were then murdered.[66]

What Bivens uncovers is that the extermination project in Indonesia became a model for the US covert operations in Latin and Central America. "Jakarta," the capital of Indonesia, in this new sinister vocabulary of political oppression, became the code word for massacre of civilians. In Brazil, Operação Jacarta became the modus operandi of the military junta. In 1971, in eastern parts of Santiago, up in the hills where many supporters of President Salvador Allende lived, a short message was plastered on the walls. "Jakarta se acerca" ("Jakarta is Coming")! Or sometimes, simply, "Jakarta."[67]

I do not intend to provide an exhaustive list of atrocities committed by the US around the world in the name of democracy, in defense of freedom. I bring this up to insist that Black Americans will not

---

65 https://nsarchive.gwu.edu/project/indonesia-documentation-project

66 Vincent Bevins, "How 'Jakarta' Became the Codeword for US-Backed Mass Killing," *The New York Review*, May 18, 2020.

67 Ibid.

be recognized as equal citizens so long as people of color around the world remain subjected to the brutality of imperialized nations such as the US. The drones that kill the Iraqi, Yemeni, Pakistani, Somali civilians, the bombs, the fighter jets, the missiles and guns that are sold to the tyrants, they are all parts of the same system of oppression that brutalizes Black Americans. The Palestinians know the meaning of ghettoization in US cities. The immigrants who are dehumanized by ICE understand the depth of police brutality and the meaning of murder with impunity. These voices need to hear one another. Black America has given voice to a global movement.

18
The Center Cannot Hold: Biden and the Challenge for Progressives

November 2020

The election is over and Trump, with or without conceding, will leave the White House. The jubilant Democrats cheer on the president-elect as he convenes his center-right administration. The disaster of four more years of Trumpogarchy was indeed incomprehensible. Having the old, corrupt party machine back in power has never felt this good.

The centrist and corporate Democrats were quick to gloat and declare themselves vindicated. They had, after all, resisted the progressives' call from inside the party to mobilize the electorate around a social-democratic agenda on labor, healthcare, education, and environment. "The progressives said we need a base candidate," said Rahm Emanuel. "No, we didn't. We needed someone to get swing voters. If you campaign appropriately, you can make that a governing transformation."[68] That the former White House Chief of Staff under President Obama and former mayor of Chicago, whose own 2015 reelection hinged on his cover-up of the police murder of the seventeen-year-old Laquan McDonald, designated himself party spokesperson was telling.[69] The obsession with the swing voter has plagued the Democrats for many decades. They continue to ignore the basic predicament of electoral politics in the US: on average, less than 50 percent of eligible voters participate in major elections. The foundational rift in the party's electoral strategy lies there. The progressives argue that the only path forward is to tap into the marginalized 50 percent, the others are resolved to hold the increasingly untenable center.

Winning the White House in an election in which by all accounts Democrats performed abysmally has deepened the rift in the party. In a widely publicized phone conversation with the members of the House Democratic Caucus, Abigail Spanberger, who represents the 7th Congressional District in Virginia, derided the "liberal" wing of the party for promoting radical ideas at the expense of winning local elections. Spanberger, who barely survived her reelection in her district, was adamant that "We need to not ever use the words 'socialist' or 'socialism' ever again because

68 https://www.nytimes.com/2020/11/09/us/politics/democratic-party-joe-biden.html

69 https://www.washingtonpost.com/national/health-science/new-questions-for-emanuel-on-what-he-knew-about-teen-shot-16-times-by-chicago-police/2016/01/14/87f326c6-bb09-11e5-99f3-184bc379b12d_story.html

while people think it doesn't matter, it does matter. And we lost good members because of that."[70]

The more vocal members of the progressive caucus, representatives such Alexandria Ocasio-Cortez (NY), Rashida Tlaib (MI), and Pramila Jayapal (WA), have rejected the centrists' blame game, reminding their colleagues that it was the massive campaign of progressive organizers that energized a dormant electorate to hand a victory to Biden.[71] The future of the party does not hinge on appeasing white middle-class suburbia.

The Democratic party machine gears up to restore the same old order that has given us Trump and the ideology on which he rode to the White House. The centrists failed in 2016 and fail today to acknowledge that one of the core elements driving Trumpism is a popular anti-establishment sensibility. Yes, Trumpism rides on racism, misogyny, and corporate greed that informs this anti-establishment movement. But partly what fuels this movement is the Republicans exceptional ability to frame the collapse of US cities and the failure of the state to fulfill its responsibilities in racial/cultural terms. By doing so, they have turned the *consequences* of naked capitalism into the *cause* of its insolvency.

The center that Democrats intend to restore will not hold. This nation cannot face the unfolding environmental catastrophe, the

---

70 https://www.washingtonpost.com/video/politics/spanberger-criticizes-democrats-strategy-in-caucus-call/2020/11/05/6ec2b368-258a-4061-9738-d83ee8971c3c_video.html

71 https://www.washingtonpost.com/politics/house-democrats-pelosi-election/2020/11/05/1ddae5ca-1f6e-11eb-90dd-abd0f7086a91_story.html

unbridled accumulation of wealth in the hands of the few, the disintegration of the infrastructure of social welfare (epitomized in the devastation brought by the COVID-19 pandemic), and the emboldened terror networks of white supremacy with haphazard measures and realignment of already existing institutions of power. Without a radical restructuring, we need to anticipate the second coming of Trump, this time not clownish, incompetent, and rash, but forceful, rational, and organized, closer in form to its fascist core.

Corporate Democrats along with their Republican colleagues have always been advocates of the doctrine of "there is no alternative" (TINA), most passionately advocated by Margaret Thatcher in the 1980s. TINA has now become the age-old wisdom of both parties in the US. A wisdom that makes thinking beyond capitalism and skepticism about its unforgiving survival of the fittest ideology socialist heresies that supposedly delegitimizes any political campaign. Socialism, particularly after WWII, became an effigy with no place in the party of the New Deal. *Amor fati,* love your destiny as you can't change it.

The Republicans and many Democrats were successful in turning the campaign of the progressive wing of the Democrats as the return of socialism. Universal health care, free education, basic income, debt forgiveness, taxing the rich, and all other reformist plans became symbols of how socialists have hijacked the party and how they plan to turn the country into another Venezuela (now gone is the day that the US was going to be turned into the Soviet Union). From an issue of well-being of all people, those against universal health care, Republicans and Democrats, turned it into a question of liberty, freedom to choose your own provider, even if you can't afford one. This project is not new. Since the time that Medicare was introduced in the 1940s, the same battle has been fought between those who consider health care a business opportunity and those who regard it as an inalienable right.

Today social media has far expanded the scope of those propaganda tools such as the Operation Coffee Cup[72] in the 1960s, when members of the American Medical Association, almost exclusively white men, asked their wives to organize gatherings for acquaintances to listen to an LP called Ronald Reagan Speaks Out Against Socialized Medicine.[73] The guests were then asked to write letters to their representatives asking them to stop the dreaded socialist plot. At the end of the recording, which in many ways launched his political career, Reagan is heard warning that "if you don't write the letter, I promise you that this program will pass as surely as the sun will come up tomorrow, and behind it there will come other federal programs that will invade every area of freedom we know in this country. Until, as Norman Thomas has said, we will awake to find that we have socialism. And if you don't do this, if I don't do it, one of these days you and I are going to spend our sunset years telling our children and our children's children what it once was like in America when men were free."

That fight continues. In 2018, on the occasion of the 200th anniversary of Karl Marx's birthday (yes, even the White House had to acknowledge that!), the Council of Economic Advisors of the Trump White House published a Report on Socialism warning that "socialism is making a comeback in American political discourse.

72 https://www.huffpost.com/entry/operation-coffeecup-reaga_b_45444

73 https://www.youtube.com/watch?v=AYrlDlrLDSQ

Detailed policy proposals from self-declared socialists are gaining support in Congress and among much of the younger electorate." The sophomoric report returns to the basic Republican caricature of socialism: a regime of taxes and spending that thrives on hampering choice and inhibiting the spirit of entrepreneurship—a recipe, the report declares, for economic disaster and loss of freedom.[74]

Centrist Democrats share that sentiment. They find common cause with Republicans in their fear of the socialist domino effect. Most often, the party leadership distances itself from any socialist project by marking it as an ill-conceived electoral strategy. This is dishonest. The leadership and the corporatist majority in the party reject socialist projects not because they are unpopular, but more importantly because those radical transformative plans do not align with interests they represent. A recent poll has shown that 57 percent of Democrats see socialism positively.[75] This number can easily and quickly grow if, rather than distancing themselves from them, Democrats begin to claim social-democratic reforms. That will not drive the party to the fringes of American politics. Let's remember that Collin Kaepernick very quickly became a persona non grata when he kneeled during the national anthem in the NFL's 2016 season. Today, all around the world, kneeling in protest against social injustice and racism has become an official part of any major athletic competition. Only two years ago, Black Lives Matter was far from the kind of respected and recognized movement for social justice that it

---

74 https://trumpwhitehouse.archives.gov/wp-content/uploads/2018/10/The-Opportunity-Costs-of-Socialism.pdf

75 https://news.gallup.com/poll/240725/democrats-positive-socialism-capitalism.aspx

is today. Universal healthcare became a seriously debated program and a central point of division among Democrats' presidential candidates, a remarkable departure from its previously non-starter status during the conversations around Obamacare. Movements and ideas need to be claimed by those who subscribe to them, otherwise they remain marginal and fade. Parties and organizations need to assert ownership of those ideas in order to make them a part of the public conversation not taboos to be eschewed.

The center cannot hold. With their centrist dream, the corporate Democrats are paving the way for the total collapse of democratic principles in the country. The next fascist president will be a competent, organized, and banal Trump, far more dangerous, far more effective. The progressives, inside and outside of the party, need to promote an agenda that will make tangible and immediate transformation in the lives of the disenfranchised and marginalized communities around the country. Let's make elections relevant to their lives.

Here is a proposal that brings all the aspects of the progressive agenda together:

A PROGRESSIVE AGENDA

Green New Deal (GND):

1. Net-zero emission by 2050.
2. Federal investment in renewable energy research and production.
3. Federal investment in new means of transportation with the goal of reduction in carbon emission (i.e. high-speed trains, zero emission public transportation, and electric cars).

4. Ban on logging and construction in federally protected lands.
5. Implementing and strengthening safe water and clean air regulations.
6. Transparency in identifying toxic waste sites.

Social Justice Projects:

1. Redistributive Plans:
    a. Universal basic income.
    b. Progressive income taxation: 0-60% without loopholes and deductions.
    c. Wealth and capital gain tax of 50%.
2. Free universal healthcare.
3. Six months of pregnancy leave (three months before and three months after childbirth). Childcare assistance for families with financial needs. Free pre-K enrollment.
4. Free primary and secondary education in addition to two-year college degree. No federal or state funds for private primary and secondary schools. Equal funding (adjusted for the cost of living) for all public primary and secondary schools.
5. Priority hiring from underrepresented communities for the implementation of the GND.
6. Federal assistance for job training and placement for historically underrepresented communities.
7. Local, state, and federal assistance in public housing toward zero homelessness.
8. Labor laws that guarantee:
    a. The right to collective bargaining.
    b. Two-week paid vacation.

   c. Sick-leave and family-leave without retribution.
   d. Maternity and/or paternity leave of a minimum three months.
9. Reinforcement and strengthening of health and safety regulations at work.

Political Reform and Regulations of Governance

1. Abolish Electoral College system.
2. Hold all elections on a holiday.
3. Restore voting rights for the incarcerated.
4. Institute new campaign reform policies to:
5. Finance presidential campaigns only through public funds.
6. Ban contributions of over $1000 to any political campaign.
7. Reverse Citizens United vs. FEC.
8. Congressional term limit.
9. Ban lobbyists employment in the government.
10. Ban former government employees to work as lobbyists.

Policing and Military Industrial Complex

1. Abolish the prison industrial complex.
2. Dissolve police departments into a Community Safety and Security Administration.
3. Abolish the military industrial complex:
   a. Cut the defense budget in half.
   b. No arms sales to other countries.
   c. No private contracts for the development of new weapons and other instruments of war.
   d. No private contractors and mercenary organizations for military supplies and missions.

International Responsibilities and Treaties

1. Respect and abide by all international norms and treaties regarding the rights of refugees and other immigrants.
2. Respect other nations' sovereignty and their rights to self-determination.
3. Stop all forms of interference in domestic affairs of other nations.
4. No imposition of economic regulations on behalf of global corporate interests.
5. No political influence to determine forms of governance.
6. Make the US subject to the international conventions, such as the International Criminal Court, that make all nations accountable for their global actions.
7. Abolish the veto power of the five countries in the United Nations.
8. Democratize the governing bodies of the World Bank and the International Monetary Fund.

19
What's the Matter with the US of A?

November 2024

As the Democrats lick their wounds after the resounding defeat of Kamala Harris, the main question remains how did this country get here? Make America Great Again captured the misogyny and racist impulse of those Americans who felt suffocated by the liberal impetus for diversity—a corporate diversity oblivious toward social justice and redistributive politics. The concomitant rise of neoliberalism in the early 1980s with multi-culturalism and the recognition of difference, what the MAGA movement dubbed wokeism, created the perception that the two are linked. The more both Democrats (particularly the Clintonians) and Republicans fostered neoliberal policies to dismantle the welfare state and to expand the corporatization of politics, media, education, healthcare, etc., the deeper the acrimony of the disenfranchised toward the entire political establishment.

Since early 1980s, the American far-right has been successful in shaping the narrative of what was unfolding in the country. They worked at the grassroot levels, municipal politics, school districts, and churches, became the spaces through which they advanced their platform. They successfully established a zero-sum game narrative between the federal and activist interventions in diversity, inclusion, women's rights, rights of the "Other" (the black, the immigrant, the queer), and the collapse of the mythical American dream, the land of opportunity and freedom.

A majority of Americans identify the political and corporate establishment *in toto* as the main culprit of what is wrong with American society. The grievances vary, but the white supremacist far-right has given them a common voice glazed with age-old ideologies of hate and antipathy. Trump has become the hero of the working class and the disenfranchised because they see in him the power to dismantle the establishment that has failed to protect them against the onslaught of deindustrialization. Trump and his allies have been successful in turning the grievances against the tribulations of neoliberalism, naked corporate power and bleak futures, into a xenophobic platform for emancipation from the tyranny of the state.

The far-right has been successful in turning "regulations" into the enemy of the people, a discursive coup that binds together corporate executives and labor. They reframed environmental regulations, labor rights laws, equal opportunity clause, and all other progressive measures as policies that forced deindustrialization and flight of capital in addition to rising consumer prices and inflation. The anti-regulation coalition razed class distinctions and unified an entire population who saw themselves as victims of the existing political order.

Although the alt-right laid the groundwork to become ideologically hegemonic, it lacked the opportunity to intervene at the federal level. That changed when in 2008, John McCain chose, albeit reluctantly, Sarah Palin as his running mate in his campaign for Presidency. This was the first time that the disgruntled anti-establishment politics found a representative at the federal level. Palin ran a campaign of ignorance-as-a-virtue, the voice of common folks who are tired of intellectual, political elites deciding on how they should run their lives, what they can and what they can't say. McCain's discomfort with Palin's outlandish, idiosyncratic populism marred the campaign with unwieldly strategy. Although McCain lost the election, this was a remarkable win for the alt-right. With Palin, they brought the supremacist discourse to the mainstream of American politics. They realized the possibility of entering federal politics and reshaping the national discourse above and beyond municipal politics of the earlier three decades.

Obama's election distorted the picture of race in American politics. The alt-right used the concept of "color-blind America" to launch coordinated campaigns to end preferential programs that resulted from the civil rights movement. Ironically, the alt-right reappropriated Dr. King's dream to "live in a nation where they will not be judged by the color of their skin but by the content of their character," in order to construct a new racist ideology for the liberation of the white nation from the tyranny of the minorities. They identified the federal government as the agent of that tyranny.

The Republicans were quick to realize that a battle between the establishment and anti-establishment political forces was unfolding. The Democrats believed that they could continue to hold the paradoxical position of being the agents of change and maintaining the existing state and corporate establishment. These two views came into direct conflict during the 2016 presidential election between Trump and Hillary Clinton. The Democrats used all their might to derail Bernie Sanders' campaign to stop him from winning the nomination of the party. Sanders ran a campaign of anti-establishment as an outsider within. He energized millions of younger generations who otherwise remained ambivalent toward electoral politics. The party elites (the Clintons, Biden, Obama, Schumer, Pelosi, and the whole class of the old guard) resented Sanders, both for his progressive socialist agenda and his anti-establishment rhetoric. They made sure that Hillary Clinton won the nomination, thinking that the establishment had to be defended. They were wrong.

Trump situated himself as the voice of the unheard. The voice of all those whose desires for the golden days of patriarchal, Jim Crow America, were checked through civic institutions and litigation. He drew big crowds to his rallies. His followers admired their newly found leader for his blunt and offensive language, *he's not afraid to say what he thinks.* A growing mass of people found that liberating. For that, they gave him the White House. The more Trump's opposition tried to portray him as a flamboyant, offensive, criminal who does not play by the rule, the wider his support became.

Trump lost the 2020 election to COVID, not to Biden. The Democrats deployed the same strategy in the 2020 primaries to make sure they nominate someone from the center of the party establishment. Facing another anti-establishment insurgency from within the party with Sanders and the progressive women caucus in the House, Obama and the rest of Democratic party dynasty came out of woodwork to restore the old order by pushing Biden to the top of the ticket. The Trump administration's utter failure in coping with the economic and social consequences of COVID cost the Republicans the presidency. Yes, the election was stolen, not by the Democrats, but by COVID.

The Democrats are slow learners. They failed to see that Biden was incapable of resisting another Trump onslaught. Despite pressures from the rank-and-file, the same old guard refused to have an open primary and nominate an alternative to Biden. But the first presidential debate at the end of June 2024 sealed the fate of Biden. It placed his cognitive decline in the open, humiliating him and the party.

His withdrawal from the candidacy opened a new window for a growing grassroots participation in the election. Harris, just for not being Biden, energized a new generation of the populace who were ready to take the election fight to every corner of every city and town in the country. The defense of reproductive rights and a fast-growing anti-war movement against the Israeli atrocities in Palestine were the two central issues that galvanized the new comers into the political scene. Harris's earlier insinuations that she would part ways with Biden's appeasement policy toward Israel encouraged the anti-war constituents to rally around her candidacy. But in August, the Party refused to allow any pro-Palestinian speaker to address the convention in Chicago.

The Convention dampened the enthusiasm and deflated all that excitement about Harris's candidacy. Harris was to become the second act of the Hillary Clinton campaign. She moved with an unprecedented speed toward proving that she was the candidate of the establishment. She secured endorsements from the military generals, intelligence chiefs, noble prize-winning economists, influential Republicans, one after another lined up to assure the public that Harris represents the old guard. Did it matter to the general public that Harris had earned the endorsement of the entire political elite, the military establishment, the Israeli lobby, and other corporate interests who were wary of Trump's unpredictability and anti-democratic posture? Did the assurances that the US would continue to support Israel unconditionally, even in the midst of an ongoing genocide, or that the NATO would defend Ukraine until the end of time mobilize anyone on her behalf?

The same strategy that led them to lose to Trump, calling him a rouge anti-establishment, convicted felon, the one who disrespects the laws of the land, combined with Harris's rush to the right, created the fate accompli of losing the presidential election. The more time they spent courting Nikki Haley constituencies the deeper the rift became between her campaign and all the potential voters whose genuine enthusiasm she crushed at the Convention. It is a mistake to think that the only effect of Harris's militarism and complacency in the genocide of Palestinians was the loss of Arab-Muslim votes in the election. Her surrender to the Israeli lobby had a much bigger significance that showed her unwillingness to step into a new political landscape, with new actors and new horizons.

For now, Trumpism has appropriated the anti-establishment sentiments in American politics. That was not inevitable, the Democrats made it so.

SECTION IV

DISSENT AND PROTEST IN IRAN

The Islamic Republic has witnessed many different forms of social unrest and political dissent across its four and a half decades of existence. The bloody first decade of the revolution gave way to a steady expansion of civil society and new forms of social and political engagement. New intellectual circles emerged, labor, and women's movements flourished. One of the major events that drew considerable attention in the past few years was the movement knows as "Women, Life, Liberty." In contrast to what most analyses of that movement have proposed, I have argued that the women's movement in Iran did not emerge from a patriarchal system that locked them up at homes without any reasonable possibility of social mobility. In these essays, I argue that women gained unprecedented social mobility after the revolution in Iran, despite patriarchal laws and other social and political restrictions, including the imposition of compulsory *hijab*. Without that level of mobility these women's movements could not materialize.

20
A Death on the Anniversary of the Iranian Revolution

February 2021

Haleh Lajevardi, an Iranian professor of sociology, died last week in Tehran at the age fifty-six. Her brother who tweeted the news of her passing did not reveal the cause of death. People close to her knew that she had dealt with bouts of depression for many years, particularly after she was dismissed from her position at Tehran University more than ten years ago.

Lajevardi was educated inside the country and received her Ph.D. from Tehran University in political theory. Her brilliance was noted when the same department that granted her degree hired her as an assistant professor after she submitted her doctoral dissertation. In addition to her own scholarship, she established herself as an influential public intellectual with her work at *Arghanun,* a journal dedicated to literary criticism, philosophy, art critique, and political theory.

From 1995 to 2006, as a board member, she regularly contributed to the journal by careful translations of texts by theorists who influenced her own work. The long list of her translations include works by Theodor Adorno, Herbert Marcuse, Richard Rorty, Paul Ricoeur, Hand Georg Gadamer, Paul Valéry, and many others. She played a key role in introducing a whole new generation of Iranians to critique as an intellectual vocation.

It is her most lasting contribution that makes her passing relevant to the anniversary of the revolution—her book *Zendegi-ye ruzmarreh dar Iran-e modern* (*Everyday Life in Modern Iran*) (2010). The book, which was based on her dissertation, is a critical look at transformation in the everyday life of Iranians, particularly that of women's, two decades after the revolution of 1979. She wrote about a period of postrevolutionary life when people of all walks of life tried to establish a sense of normalcy and order outside the revolutionary fervor and devastations of war.

Through a close reading of a number of Iranian films that follow the lives of ordinary people in different social milieus, Lajevardi investigates how the heroic life of revolutionary times is translated into the monotony of everyday routines. Describing a scene from *Under the Skin of the City,* a film by Rakhshan Bani-Etemad, one of the most prolific Iranian women filmmakers, Lajevardi shows how Tuba, an old working-class woman, has become a subject fully conscious of her being and her place in her social world. Tuba knows how and why she should assert herself in the realities of her daily life, at home, at work, in the neighborhood, with her family, with the filmmaker who is following her moves.

This, for Lajevardi, was the most significant consequence of the revolution. The revolution spread the idea of sovereignty across the country—the idea that not only do we have the right of self-determination as a nation, but also as individuals we have the ability and the authority to exercise our will over our circumstances.

She wrote her book during the decade that saw the rise of civil society, during the time that a new generation of Iranians looked inward in the hopes of realizing the possibilities of foundational transformations and social change. Lajevardi saw herself as one of the subjects of her study. She understood the experience of individual sovereignty as "a walk on the razor's edge."

I do not know whether she chose "the razor's edge" in that passage in her book as a reference to Somerset Maugham's novel. But her anxieties in her book about the tension between self-consciousness and one's real possibilities in life, between hope and despair recall the epigraph in Maugham's book: "The sharp edge of a razor is difficult to pass over; thus the wise say the path to Salvation is hard."

The edge of the razor was not kind to Lajevardi. She was dismissed from her job after the massive protests over the results of the presidential election in 2009. Everyday life became a struggle for the scholar of everyday life. A thick layer of despair and depression stifled the prospects of hope and jubilance.

In a note on the passing of Haleh Lajevardi, one of her colleagues Abbas Kazemi wrote, "Hope had sprouted on campus [when she was there] during the reform era. Massive waves of change formed gently and rose to encompass our entire lives. Then the waves quietly ceased, swallowed by the earth not to return ever again. Amazing human beings who faded and died, many of whom we do not know their names, gone in despair in an everlasting migration."[76]

Revolutions are walks on the edge of a razor, a bloody venture into a world that promises hope and faces despair—the hope of *possible realities* and the despair of facing *real possibilities*. Haleh Lajevardi saw with true brilliance that the everyday life of a nation will not be the same after undergoing a historic revolution. Everyday life might cease to be heroic, but it transforms the ordinary into something self-conscious. She knew that the revolution would continue to live in that sovereign subject, the ordinary person who is aware of her authority and ability to determine her own fate.

76 https://www.independentpersian.com/node/124636/%D8%AF

It is a sad occasion to celebrate the anniversary of the revolution without one of those who recognized its historic significance. A young cultural theorist who shined light on the gift of self-determination that was bestowed upon Iranians by a revolutionary movement that transformed individuals into conscious, hope-bearing subjects. The current rulers of the country need to recognize that such despair undermines the legitimacy of their rule. Despair is a malaise that threatens the sovereignty of the country. Many people have left the train of the revolution since its inception, many have stepped down and others thrown out. But today there are expectations that need to be realized, demands that need to be met, and voices that need to be heard.

Last year on the anniversary of the revolution President Rouhani warned that "the previous regime fell in 1979 because it failed to recognize the voices of the people." All factions in the Iranian state need to take that lesson to heart. People who make their voices heard might be silenced, some like Lajevardi might fall into absolute despair, some others might leave for exile, some might romanticize life before the revolution, some might even promote debilitating US sanctions imposed on the whole nation as a wake-up call. But would those in power want to rule a nation rent in despair? Let us hope that these beautiful voices are heard, even in their eternal absence.

21

Doshman and the Massive Protests in Iran

October 2022

After a stunning silence through two weeks of public protest and state violence, the Supreme Leader of the Islamic Republic, Ayatollah Khamenei delivered a spiteful attack on those who have been protesting on the streets of Tehran and many other major cities in the country.[77] He called the protests, which began after the death of Mahsa Amini in police custody and soon became widespread, the result of a conspiracy by Western powers to overthrow the Islamic Republic. "*Doshman* (the enemy)," he repeated his tired rhetoric, "had plans to destabilize the country and used the unfortunate death of this young woman as a pretext to instigate conflict and sedition." Laying the blame exclusively at the feet of the *Doshman* (the US, its regional allies, and their domestic agents) has been the Supreme

77 https://www.aparat.com/v/95HN1

Leader's go-to move in addressing social unrest in Iran since he took office after the death of Ayatollah Khomeini in 1989. That he chose to break his public silence in a speech to an audience at an Armed Forces graduation ceremony was telling. So was his nationalist rhetoric, side-stepping the deep causes of internal dissent. The *Doshman* he told his audience, "is not only against the Islamic Republic, they are against a strong and independent Iran. *Doshman* wants to install a client state in our country that acts on behalf of their regional interests, not the interests of Iranian peoples." Commenting on why these protests transpired at this particular moment, he contended that "the unrest was designed to coincide with Iran's great leap forward toward economic progress despite the hardships that the Western powers impose upon us."

These are strong words, yet without much traction in the Iranian scene. The presence of *Doshman* is real, but he offers wrong reasons for the expansion of its influence inside the country. There are four major issues that the Supreme Leader conveniently erases from his narrative of *Doshman's* conspiracy. One, if he is correct that the protests are a *Doshman* conspiracy, why is it so easy for them to foment unrest inside the country? Why is it that Iranian society, with women and youth at the lead, has been a tinderbox for the past two decades? Second, he does not address the question of how these protests so easily move, according to him, toward fulfilling the interests of the *Doshman*? Why is it that there are no parties, no organizations, no leadership in these rallies, a vacant space that allows the *Doshman* to influence the direction and demands of the protesters? Third, the deepening gap between the rich and poor and the skyrocketing rate of inflation, particularly during the past few months, cannot be erased simply by a sermon touting a "great leap forward" of all things. The pain of economic hardship is real and needs real solutions rather than wishful slogans. Lastly, the Supreme Leader dismissed the public solidarity of athletes and artists with the protesters as "worthless and irrelevant." He fails utterly to recognize why after more than four decades of Islamic rule, the influence of the captain of the Iranian national soccer team or an Oscar winning film director are significantly greater than the imams of Friday prayers.

The Iranian society continues to witness a deep rift between the state and its citizens. The median age of the population is 32, close to 80 percent of Iranians were born after the revolution and have no recollection of life before the revolution of 1979. The Supreme Leader's rhetoric that the protesters were "families of SAVAK agents" (the Shah's secret police) falls flat on this generation's face. It is instead an implicit admission that the Islamic Republic has failed to grow and accommodate the needs and demands of its population. The laws and restrictions that were instituted more than forty years ago failed to shape the worldview and desires of a generation that grew up under this system as intended. The Supreme Leader needs to acknowledge the Islamic Republic's failure to invent a narrowly conceived *homo islamicus,* receptive and accommodating to the ethos and values propagated by a clerical establishment.

The misogynist core of that project, expressed in a restrictive reading of Islamic juridical tradition in inheritance, marriage and children's custody, and *hijab,* continues to alienate and impede millions of Iranian women from political processes in the country. Billions of dollars have been spent in education, cultural production, and social tutelage to realize the ambitious Islamization projects that has only produced the opposite of their intended objectives. There is something painfully wrong if the religious mandate of *al-amr bi-l-maʿrūf wa-n-nahy ʿani-l-munkar* (Enjoin the good and forbid the wrong) must be enforced by the patrolling police officers after decades of mandating teachers, state-owned media, radio-television, and preachers with billions of dollars budget failed to advance this project. This is a familiar story, a regime fails to become hegemonic, and resorts to naked coercion. Coercion breathes discontent and violence, a tinderbox.

Since the establishment of the Islamic Republic, voices of dissent, inside and outside the polity, have been suppressed systematically and punitively. A certain space for conversation remains open in the independent media, publishing world, and in intellectual circles. But the state has seldom shown patience for the institutionalization of those voices in political parties and civil society organizations. The absence of such institutional means of dissent inevitably forces the populace to express any form of grievances through street politics. The lack of institutional representation further diminishes the state's ability to mitigate the spread of violence. Once a state murders, exiles, jails, and puts under house arrest oppositional voices, it rubs itself from the possibility of a meaningful engagement with the demands of its citizens. *A state that eliminates dissidents and oppositional parties is solely responsible if the* Doshman *exploits and instrumentalizes a leaderless protest.*

The Supreme Leader speaks of the success of the administration of President Raisi in containing the economic crisis that has led to an unprecedented inflation and deepening the gap between the haves and have nots in Iran. All the official numbers contradict the

Supreme Leader's claim. The idea that the *Doshman* conspired to foment unrest in order to through Iran off track from its economic successes and from overcoming the devastating effects of American sanctions will not stand even a cursory scrutiny. President Raisi was elected, after all his major opponents were disqualified from running by the Guardian Council, with the promise of curbing the inflation and bringing it down to single digits. Since his inauguration in August 2021, the inflation rate has doubled to 54% with the prices of basic goods increasing even on a faster pace.[78]

The increase in prices of basic goods at the first anniversary of Mr. Raisi's election was reported in *Etemad* newspaper in Tehran: Chicken: 101%; Lamb: 41%; Rice (domestic): 200%; Vegetable oil: 367%; Eggs: 114%; Pasta: 168%; Butter: 120%; Yoghurt: 185%; Cheese: 133%; Sugar: 102%; Milk: 99%; Internet services: 101%.

These are numbers that are published by Iran's own Central Bank and the Statistical Center of Iran. They are available to the Supreme Leader who unfortunately does not go shopping, hence removed from the real pain of this economic hardship. His comments on upward trajectory of living conditions in Iran deepen peoples' mistrust of the government and further encourages them to voice their grievances directly on the streets rather than seeking bureaucratic and administrative solutions.

78 https://tradingeconomics.com/iran/inflation-cpi

Here the Supreme Leader had the opportunity to highlight how the unjust sanctions imposed by the *Doshman* had devastating effects and how it has harmed the ordinary people in the country. But to do so, he needed to acknowledge that the sanctions had made the concentration of wealth on the top Iranian 1 percent greater than ever. Iranians have shown that they are willing to brave the difficulties of all kinds of foreign pressures, but they cannot bear to witness the suffering of a great majority while a small minority profits from circumventing the sanctions. Sanction profiteers inside the country are allies of those who impose those draconian, debilitating sanctions on Iran.

The Supreme Leader's derogatory comments on celebrities, actors, athletes are a slap in the face to the brave public and will further antagonize crowds on the streets. This is another indicator of how alienated the regime has become from the realities of Iranian society. The celebrities did not author the chant *Women, Life, Freedom,* they only echo it, like the rest of the world. The chant comes from the depth of a multifaceted form of resistance that is tired of old plans and worn-out visions of the future. It is a potentiality put forward by those who stand at the threshold of a novelty, like those who stood at the same point during the revolution of 1979.

The revolutionary spirit that lingers in Iran remains bewildering. The courage, the fearlessness with which young women claim the streets, and the hope that is espoused in the piercing chants of *Women, Life, Freedom,* need to be embraced and encouraged, without reservation. The brutality of the police and the carceral state must be exposed and condemned without hesitation. At the same time, I believe, it must be recognized that no gesture of solidarity or condemnation happens in a political vacuum. In this trajectory, the geo-politics of Iran, remapping the Middle East and extending the American and its regional allies influence, and the effects of the violent crippling sanctions against imposed on Iran cannot be ignored. *Doshman* is real.

The Supreme Leader is right to emphasize that a central problem of the *Doshman* is Iran's sovereignty, a treasure that was earned through the pains of revolution. He fails, however, to accept the idea that not only do we have the right of self-determination as a nation, but also as individuals and communities we have the ability and the authority to exercise our will over our circumstances. *A sovereign nation will not last without sovereign subjects.*

Let us hope that supporting the protests in Iran and the condemnation of the state's brutality will generate a new political space in which the chant of *women, life, freedom* is heard without being appropriated by those who would instrumentalize it for their own gains. This movement has already realized significant achievements. It has shaken the dominant discourses of ruling classes on women's rights and civil liberties. For the first time since the revolution, open discussions are happening on primetime state television,[79] among the parliamentarians,[80] at the university administrative offices, etc. on the wisdom of compulsory *hijab* and on the failure of the project of *enjoin the good and forbid the wrong* in the hands of the so-called morality police.

The success or failure of these protests must not be tied to regime change. The exercise of sovereignty on the streets in a success, pushing the boundaries of permissible and forbidden is a success, the display of courage and global solidarity is a success, not seeing all these achievements is a failure. More than a decade ago, the late Haleh Lajevardi (see Chapter 20), compared the experience of individual sovereignty as "a walk on the razor's edge." I do not know

79 https://www.youtube.com/watch?v=RxH-B5gL3yU

80 At the time, the current Iranian president, Masoud Pezeshkian, was a member of the parliament. He spoke vociferously to call for transparency and an end to the draconian enforcement of mandatory *hejāb*.

whether she chose "the razor's edge" in that passage in her book as a reference to Somerset Maugham's novel. But her anxieties about the tension between self-consciousness and one's real possibilities in life, between hope and despair recall the epigraph in Maugham's book "The sharp edge of a razor is difficult to pass over; thus the wise say the path to Salvation is hard." "The path to Salvation" in Iran will not be paved by the American government, Israeli agents, and the Saudi interests. Iranian women, all Iranians, do not need to be "saved" by foreign intervention, by sanctions or any other means. They have shown their sovereign power again and again for more than a century, they are the teachers. We all need to take a page from these courageous women's book and resist the temptations to shake the hands of those whose objective is to instrumentalize these protests to advance their geo-political ambitions.

These protests are walks on the edge of a razor, a bloody venture into a world that promises hope and faces despair. Strapping these protests to regime change ties the rebellious subject to an *all or nothing* trajectory that promises despair rather than cultivating hope.

22

How the Islamic Revolution Gave Rise to a Massive Women's Movement in Iran

November 2022

Let me start with a straightforward proposition that is everywhere on social and mass media these days: The Islamic Republic's patriarchal repression of women reached a tipping point after the murder in custody of Mahsa (Zhina) Amini by the Guidance Patrol on September 16, 2022. A revolt, led by young women, engulfed the entire country under the banner of *women, life, freedom.* At the root of this movement is the anti-women core of the Islamic regime and the struggle of Iranian women against it since its very beginning in 1979. The whole nation — inside and outside the country, the global community, the progressive Left as well as the hawkish Right, stand in solidarity with this movement. The protests that began against the compulsory *hijab* and the demand for abolishment of the Guidance Patrol, has now become a full-fledged intersectional revolt for regime change in Iran, led by women.

This indeed is true that the Islamic Republic instituted draconian patriarchal policies after the revolution on 1979 that stripped the very basic formal rights that women had been granted under the *ancien régime.* These measures formally reduced women to second-class citizens in matters of marriage, custody, inheritance, crime and judiciary, dress code, segregation, and many other spheres of social life. Yet, despite all this, women's social mobility and presence in public sphere grew exponentially in the past four decades. Ironically, this is in part an effect of the unintended consequences of these policies. Women learned very quickly how to navigate the new terrain, push the boundaries of the new institutions, and *in practice* gain access to rights and privileges from which the Islamic Republic deprived them. The recent revolt could not materialize without the remarkable agentive presence and mobility of women who carved out a space for ceaseless social and political engagement during the past four decades. Women are revolting because they refuse to continue the struggle in a field the boundaries of which are drawn in the dilapidated spirits of patriarchy. Their gains have reached a hard as well as a glass ceiling that needs to be overcome.

The Iranian revolution succeeded in ending the monarchy on February 11, 1979. On February 26, only two weeks after the victory of the revolution, Ayatollah Khomeini annulled the Family Protection Law of 1967 and its 1975 amended version, which had given women more rights in divorce and matters of custody under the Shah. Since its inception, the clergy by and large had opposed the law's basic premises, which they believed violated the Islamic views on women's role in family. Khomeini knew that the unity and uniformity that his leadership afforded the revolutionary movement would not remain uncontested for long after the triumph of the revolution. He knew that the spirit of Islam and the symbolic revolutionary language with which it inspired millions of Iranians of many creeds and classes needed to be translated into a body of institutional projects of postrevolutionary state-building. So, he seized the opportunity to put women under the control of their menfolk.

Despite such overt assaults on women's rights, most political parties continue to address women's issues in the frame of revolutionary politics, nationalism, class struggle, and anti-imperialism. For the first few months after the revolution, except for the National Front, the oldest liberal organization in Iran, and small Trotskyist group, Left and liberal parties remained ambivalent about women's issues. They failed to recognize the remarkable contribution of women to the revolutionary struggle and the need to check the assault on their rights. At the time, most of the women's organization operated as an appendix to different political parties to further the anti-imperialist struggle and tied women's issues to greater demands for social justice.

The establishment of the Islamic Republic proved inconsistent with fundamental women's formal and legal rights. Despite earlier assurances, on the eve of March 8, 1979, less than a month after the triumph of the revolution, Ayatollah Khomeini called upon the Provisional Government to uphold Islamic dress codes in its offices. His pronouncement scandalized many who played a significant role in the revolutionary movement, including several members of his own Revolutionary Council. This was the second time, after the abrogation of the Family Protection Law, in three weeks that issues of women's right had become a point of contention in the postrevolutionary power struggle. That was why the festive preparations for the first postrevolutionary International Women's Day turned into a rally with specific women's rights demands such as the recognition of women judges and, most importantly, a call against compulsory *hejāb*. Thousands of women gathered in Tehran University and the next day in front of and inside the hallways of the Ministry of Justice chanting: *In the Spring of freedom, absent is the rights of women.*

Instituting compulsory *hejāb* even in the tightly controlled parliament and implementing it throughout the country was not an easy proposition. It took another four years for the mandate to become an enforceable law. Different factions inside the government as well as influential clerics in seminaries raised questions about the wisdom of such a law, its religious justification, as well as its feasibility. Nevertheless, the new law went into effect on August 9, 1983.

The institution of compulsory *hejāb* and other patriarchal measures in cases of travel, marriage, custody, inheritance, criminal laws, etc. all of which formally reduced women to second-class citizens, gave yet more credibility to feminist concerns that the Islamic republic would entirely force women out of the public sphere. Comparisons were made with Reza Shah. Some argued that whereas he liberated Muslim women by the "unveiling law" that banned the *hejāb* in public spaces in 1936, the Islamic Republic was now forcing women back into the private sphere where they would be subjected to the repressive domestic patriarchy. Yet curiously – these contrasting policies produced paradoxical results on the ground. Reza Shah's "unveiling" did not liberate women, and the Islamic Republic's repressive measures did not imprison women at home. Ironically, it was under Reza

Shah's "unveiling law" that a great majority of women in urban areas were forced to stay at home, either because they chose not to appear in public without a veil or were not allowed to leave their homes by their fathers or husbands. Under the Islamic Republic, despite the institution of repressive anti-women laws, rather than being imprisoned in their homes, women gained unprecedented mobility in the country and year after year increased their presence in the public sphere.

These were unintended consequences, but they were quite substantial. As a consequence of the restrictions imposed on women in public places, a new system emerged of what I call *patriarchy by proxy*. The new laws created the possibility for a great majority of socially conservative Iranian families who were previously reluctant to see women's participation in social affairs, to trust the new "Islamized" public sphere as an extended domain of patriarchal/religious order. The state became the ultimate guardian of patriarchy and by becoming so, paradoxically, sanctioned an unprecedented mobility among rural and urban women. Despite barring women from entering key political and judicial positions of decision-making, women entered and shaped the conditions of those spheres in significant numbers.

In practice, gender politics and policy under the Islamic Republic have been far from the mere enactment of literal readings of the Qur'anic verses or a replication of women's repression in Saudi Arabia. There is no doubt that the postrevolutionary regime instituted formal and legal apparatuses in order to constitute a *homo Islamicus*. But in its *realpolitik*, the Islamic Republic negated the anxieties that it would implement a literal reading of the Qur'an and expunge women from the pubic and restrict their lives to the domestic sphere. A quick look at the human development indexes in relation to women's status in education, health, sports, artistic and cultural production, and civic engagement shows that the women in Iran have the most visible presence in public sphere in its history. These changes were not the result of top-down state policies, but rather the consequence of a contentious engagement between different factions within the polity, women's community and civic institutions, and political parties and activists.

From the time of revolution in 1979 to the latest reports in 2019, women's literacy rate rose from 36 percent to 97.93 percent share of women students in higher education rose from 15 percent to 60 percent women's life expectancy rose from 55 to 77; infant mortality decreased from 90 per 1000 to 10 per 1000. None of these could have been possible without a remarkable presence of women in public space and their involvement in policy planning and implementation.

The significant presence of women in the public arena created unanticipated shifts in gender relations in the country, conditions that forced even the most patriarchal factions in power to advocate unlikely propositions regarding women's role in society. In 2006-2007 school year, women comprised 60% of incoming class of university students, and that trend continues. The conservatives of the 8th Parliament introduced legislation for affirmative action for men to catch up with women in higher education. The conservative parliamentarians, who otherwise insist that the place of women is at home to raise a virtuous family, argued that women who use resources of free public universities had to commit to a 10-year employment (public or private) after graduation. The paradox there is self-evident.

Another measure that contributed to the remarkable shift in family structure and gendered relations in public and private spheres was an aggressive family planning and population control program that was instituted in 1989. Although the Islamic Republic repealed the family planning and protection laws of the old regime soon after assuming power, in a significant shift, in 1988, the government introduced and carried out one of the most efficient family planning programs in the economically developing world. Dictated by the perceived necessity of containing an unchecked rise in population, the program successfully reduced the population growth rate from the high of 3.4 percent in 1986 to 0.7 percent in 2007. During the same period, the number of children per family dropped from 6.5 to less than 2. Before his death in 1989, Ayatollah Khomeini endorsed the new program thus affording religious legitimacy to this ideological reversal. As the Canadian-Iranian anthropologists Homa Hoodfar has shown, without national consensus-building, a massive mobilization of women, both by government agencies as well as non-governmental agents, promoted with effective religious justification, and offered through an efficient delivery service in birth control and contraceptives (such as distribution of free condoms), and premarital sex-education programs, this ambitious family planning project could not have been realized.[81] Called by many "The Iranian Miracle,"[82] the program was so successful that, fearing the

81 Homa Hoodfar, Devices and Desires: Population Policy and Gender Roles in the Islamic Republic," *Middle East Report,* no. 190, pp. 11-17, 1994.

82 Patricia Dérer, "The Iranian Miracle: The Most Effective Family Planning Program in History," March 21, 2019, accessed: https://overpopulation-project.com/the-iranian-miracle-the-most-effective-family-planning-program-in-history/

emergence of an aging population, the authorities are now trying to encourage families to have more children.

The purpose of this brisk history is not to draw a sanguine picture of women's conditions in contemporary Iran. The complexities of how government and non-governmental actors interact on these issues, how the expansion and containment of state power shape the social realities of women of different classes and ethnicities, or how religious doctrines and convictions hinder or facilitate women's mobility cannot be fully detailed here. Rather, I want to show that the Islamic Republic instituted policies and imposed patriarchal laws that produced unintended consequences in gender relations and women's mobility. For an uprising to materialize, there needs to be a socially mobile, politically conscious, and subjectively free population. Iranian women have long been the fierce political actors we see on the street, not the oppressed, shadowy, veiled subjects that are the meat and potatoes of foreign misperception and paternalism. Yes, a mighty patriarchy shaped social order in Iran, like many other places in the world, but women were never its hapless captives. That image, the helpless veiled women, while effective in gathering support in global liberal feminist circles who believe that Muslim women need to be saved,[83] does not correspond to the practice of those women's everyday lives and fails to credit two generations of Iranian women for their political creativity.

At its core, *Women-Life-Freedom* is a movement for dignity and sovereignty of the subject. It is a movement that has changed the

---

83 For a critique of that liberal feminism see Lila Abu-Lughod, *Do Muslim Women Need Saving?* Cambridge, MA: Harvard university Press, 2015.

political culture of defiance and expressions of dissent. Its radical creativity— posters, songs, graffiti, and imaginative forms of collective action, has opened *in practice* the possibility of thinking of politics anew. The transformative acts of insubordinate bodies and liberated souls has made party platforms and unruffled sermons ineffective and obsolete.

While Iranian women and their male allies fight against the state's brutal crackdown, their aspiring revolt, with its novel singularities, faces instrumentalization by regional and global actors, facilitated through a misreading of Iranian women's history of deliberate and agentive action. While the global reach of this movement through the media operates as an instrument of its effective dissemination, paradoxically, it also subjects it to a discursive violence. We should not misread the core principles of *Women, Life, Freedom* as being a simple "desire for the west"[84] by a population who are simply fed up. Under such a misreading, a whole host of unsavory interests, from neocolonial expansionists to ethno-nationalist separatists, from delusional monarchists to all those who still lament being on the losing side of the 1979 revolution, try their best to claim ownership of this movement. Yet Iranian women on the ground have been the very actors who historically have created the conditions of possibility for their protest. They have opened space for themselves and their daughters in the face of a state desire for repressive patriarchy. Over decades they have succeeded to take advantage of the unintended

84 Alain Badiou (translated by Georgy Elliot), *The Rebirth of History: Times of Riots and Uprisings*, London: Verso, 2012.

consequences of state policies; they are not merely reacting—they are instead determined.

Today's massive women's movement in Iran represents one of the great achievements of the 1979 revolution—a revolution that generated hope-bearing, conscious subjects who have perpetuated themselves for more than four decades – despite and in the face of all manner of repression. The paradoxical effects of the Islamic Republic policies brought women to the centerstage of social transformation in Iran. Now that transformation has reached a point of frontal war with the state. Iranian women today hold key positions in journalism, artistic and cultural production, civic engagement, political organizing, higher education, scientific communities, local political offices, etc. Daughters of those women, irrevocably demand an extension and expansion of their mothers' positions without any patriarchal restrictions, either by the state or inside their homes. Those demands will only be realized through the transformation of the state, or by rethinking the meaning of the state. How this transformation will unfold and with what means is yet not known, but its inevitability is evident. How fortunate we are that these generations of women taking the lead.

23
Revolutionary Dreams, Repressive Realities

January 2023

On September 16, 2022, twenty-two-year-old Mahsa Amini died in custody in Tehran following her arrest by the Guidance Patrol (*Gasht-e Ershad*). Instantly, her death became a rallying cry for young Iranian women against the existing political order that has imposed and maintains unyielding patriarchal restrictions on women's legal rights and life choices. Captured in the mantra *Zan, Zendegi, Āzādi* ("Women, Life, Liberty"), the protests that began in Saqqez, Mahsa Amini's hometown in Iran's Kurdish north, soon became a nation-wide revolt against the Islamic Republic. The judiciary, the police, and the state-controlled media made an absurd attempt to attribute Ms. Amini's death to natural causes. But why, people asked, was a young woman in police custody for failing to observe an arbitrary dress code in the first place?

The speed with which the protests spread throughout the country and were radicalized into an anti-regime revolt surprised the government. They were ill-prepared to respond, as was evidenced in its brutal show of force on the streets and in the rapidly unfolding propaganda war inside and outside the country. Finally, after two weeks of mystifying silence, the Supreme Leader, Ayatollah Khamenei, spoke. He blamed Western powers for fomenting unrest in the country and manipulating "naïve young people" into executing a sinister plot to overthrow the Islamic Republic. He refused to acknowledge the deep and palpable discontent over a variety of issues that had motivated the unrest. The increasing pauperization of people from all walks of life (caused partly by the crippling US-led sanctions); the anguish and hopelessness of a new generation that feels deeply alienated from the culture and values that ruling classes promote; the feeling of abandonment of marginalized regions, particularly Kurdistan and Baluchistan; rampant corruption that plagues the state agencies and top officials; and many other legitimate grievances of the nation have found no place in the state's narrative of the revolts that have shaken the foundations of the Islamic Republic.

It is true that there are regional and global state actors who are trying to instrumentalize and exploit these protests in order to topple the Islamic Republic or to coerce the regime in Tehran into submitting to the demands of Western powers. But the regime's failure to acknowledge the legitimate grievances of an entire population will only deepen the protesters' antagonism and further polarize the political situation.

The ongoing uprisings in Iran might ultimately end the experiment that was Islamic Republicanism. Unlike the common analyses that attribute the current events in Iran to either the total failure of the Islamic revolution or an instance of the impossibility of the Islamic state,[85] I see the present revolt, ironically, as the realization of Islamic Republicanism. I use the term "realization" in a dialectical sense to suggest that the Islamic Republic negates itself through its own realization. In other words, the republican process—with references to teachings of Islam—unleashed massive participation of otherwise excluded social groups (particularly women) who would eventually question the dominant ideology that made that participation possible. This dialectical process began to unfold from the moment when Ayatollah Khomeini, for the first time during his exile in Paris in 1978, spoke of the establishment of an Islamic *Republic.* He made that declaration with the full consciousness of the essence of republicanism that lies in the principle of peoples' sovereignty and their right to self-determination.[86]

From the very beginning of the establishment of the Islamic Republic in 1979, the conflicting institutional sources of sovereignty and legitimacy of the state became a contested political predicament. The *Majlis* (Parliament), the office of the presidency, the prime minister's office, the office of the *velāyat-e faqih* (the guardianship of the jurist), and the Guardian Council all struggled to reconcile the sovereignty of the people with the Islamic character of the new republic. The constitution of the Islamic Republic recognized the

---

85 Wael Hallaq, *The Impossible State, Islam, Politics, and Modernity's Moral Predicament,* New York: Columbia University Press.

86 Ruhollah Khomeini, *Sahifeh-ye Imam* (*Collected Works*), Vol. 5, p. 242, speech delivered on December 16, 1978 in Paris.

right of self-determination, so long as its exercise does not contradict the principles of Islamic creeds. In practice, however, rather than a point of reference, Islam became a contested body of religious discourses with competing interpretations from inside and outside of clerical establishment. The framers of the constitution believed that once they established the *form* of governance, Islam would shape its substance. They wanted to establish a religious state by *sacralizing politics*, making Islam the point of reference for good politics; in practice they *secularized religion*,[87] making the state's expediencies the arbiter of the right interpretations of Islam. In other words, rather than a religious state, the clerical establishment created a state religion. By doing so, not only did they suppress voices of dissent from outside of the polity, but they also marginalized the seminaries and the seminarians and turned them into an appendix to the state and its interests.

The struggle over who could legitimately claim authority in interpreting Islam and its teachings on good governance gave rise to a reformist movement in the 1990s.[88] Now lay intellectuals, lawyers, journalists, women activists, young seminarians, and other social groups claimed authority in interpreting Islam and in defining the meaning of the right of self-determination and its relation to Islamic principles. The reform movement that culminated in the two-term presidency of Mohammad Khatami (1997–2005) emerged from

87 Joshua S. Lupo, "Introduction to Symposium on When Politics are Sacralized," https://contendingmodernities.nd.edu/theorizing-modernities/intro-politics-sacralized/ (September 21, 2022)

88 Behrooz Ghamari-Tabrizi, *Islam and Dissent in Postrevolutionary Iran: Religious Politics and Democratic Reform*, London: Bloomsbury, 2008.

the unintended consequence of making Islam the point of reference for good governance. The remarkable mobility of women (see the next chapter, their unprecedented access to education and health care, and their demands for equal rights,[89] particularly in the cases of divorce, children's custody, and inheritance, had a constitutive significance in this movement.

Image of large crowd taken in February 1979 after Khomeini's return to Iran from Paris. ©2023 David Burnett/Contact Press Images

Although the reformists theorized their movement on the principle of "bargaining from the top and pressuring from the bottom," for the most part, they remained a movement for participation in political power. Civil society—the publication of private newspapers,

89 Behrooz Ghamari-Tabrizi, "Women's Rights, *Shari'a* Law, and the Secularization of Islam in Iran," *International Journal of Politics, Culture, and Society,* vol. 26, pp. 237-253, June 2013.

the strong publishing industry, the formation of vibrant intellectual circles, and various forms of women's groups (reading groups, sports, professional associations)—flourished in precarious terms.[90] Nevertheless, it generated and sustained a deep sense of transformative power among people of all walks of life. Despite the omnipresence of state repression, this collective sense of empowerment and civic engagement grew rhizomatically, without a vertical hierarchical structure. The state, with its complex and oversized system of intelligence gathering and surveillance, remained suspicious of all political parties, professional associations, and other formal institutions that could possibly mobilize their constituents for any form of political and/or civil action. But these informal and loosely connected, or disconnected, networks grew exponentially among a new generation that cared little for the revolutionary mores and values that defined both the ruling classes and those who had hitherto defied them.

The economic crises that were perpetuated by the US' crippling sanctions, which had intensified during the two-term presidency of Mahmoud Ahmadinejad (2005–2013), hastened the separation and antagonism between the state and civil society. Rampant corruption

90 For example look at the following studies: Mehran Kamrava, "The Civil Society Discourse in Iran," *British Journal of Middle Eastern Studies*, vol. 28:2, pp. 165-185, 2010; Niloofar Haeri, *Say What Your Longing Heart Desires: Women, Prayer, and Poetry in Iran*, Stanford: Stanford University Press, 2022; Jenny Steel & Sophie Richter-Devroe, "The Development of Women's Football in Iran: A Perspective on the Future of Women's Sport in the Islamic Republic," *Journal of the British Institute of Persian Studies*, vol. 41:1, pp. 315-322, 2017; Roksana Bahramitash, "Revolution, Islamization, and Women's Employment in Iran," *The Brown Journal of World Affairs*, vol. 9:2, pp. 229-241.

and virulent crony capitalism, disguised as the privatization project of the state-owned industry, increasingly deepened this antagonism. To reframe this growing discontent, to justify its own patriarchal repression, the state adopted an instrumental relation with Islam, labeling all expressions of discontent conspiracies against Islam and the sovereignty of the Islamic Republic.

Since its inception, there has been a major divide within the polity of the Islamic Republic between those who advocate a totalitarian ideology that operates based on the notion of insider/outsider and friend vs. enemy, and a disappearing minority who promote something similar to an agonistic democracy.[91] The latter aims to turn enemies into adversaries and transform all antagonisms into agonism. The final nail in the coffin of the agonistic tendency was the election of Ebrahim Raisi to the presidency in 2021. Raisi prevailed in an election in which the Guardian Council disqualified all other viable candidates from running. Popular participation was the lowest in the forty-year history of the republic. The conservatives cynically seized all three branches of the government and took a major step toward the realization of their totalitarian dreams.

The Supreme Leader, along with the Guardian Council, tried in vain to delink the regime's legitimacy to electoral participation (see Chapter 5). For the first time since its inception, the absence of competing factions in elections created a clear rupture between the Islamic Republic's polity and its constituents. By monopolizing all

91 Chantal Mouffe, "Agonistic Democracy and Radical Politics," *Pavilion: Journal for Politics and Culture*, available at https://www.pavilionmagazine.org/chantal-mouffe-agonistic-democracy-and-radical-politics/

three branches of the government, the conservatives created a state that defined itself in the self/other binary terms without leaving any institutional forms for the expression of dissent for the "other."

The protests of the past few months demonstrate how this binary of self/other was translated into open hostilities and seemingly unresolvable antagonisms fought on the streets of every urban center in the country. Women stand at the forefront, driving this nationwide revolt because there exists the deepest contradiction between their massive participation in social affairs (artistic-cultural production, journalism, education, civic engagement) and the patriarchal laws and denigrating regulations that seek to govern their bodies and appearances. We do not know whether this movement will lead to regime change or a major overhaul of the existing order. Those at the top might succeed in using the uprising to entrench the authority of the Islamic Republic through a brutal reign of terror. We all hope fervently that the latter does not come to pass. But one thing is certain as Iranian women have demonstrated these past several months: A nation that has inherited a revolutionary spirit and has perpetuated it through collective expressions of discontent over the past four decades will not easily submit to naked repression, regardless of how it is exercised or justified.

SECTION V

MUSLIM VOICES AND THE MEDIA

Subtle and open Islamophobia gives legitimacy to political positions that are detrimental to Muslims around the world. Demonization of Islam and Muslims has long historical roots. But since the attacks of 9/11, it has found new and violent expression in the War on Terror and Western powers' fight to maintain their hegemony in the Middle East. Muslims are often depicted as violent, irrational, backward, misogynistic, and aggressive in public domain. They are seen as humorless and intolerant. Seldom are these depictions put in the contemporary asymmetrical relations of power. These representations often see Muslim majority societies in an undifferentiated totality without recognizing their diversities in cultures and ideas. These essays are my attempt to recognize those relations of power and how they operate in practice.

24

Lost Muslim Voices of Dissent

December 2004

In his recent book, Mahmood Mamdani called Good Muslim-Bad Muslim a fictitious dichotomy that petrifies Islam into a set of privatized beliefs without any relevance to politics or a dogmatic ideology of violence. War-planners and apologists for President Bush's "War on Terror" accept this dichotomy, with the result that the voices of Muslim critics who transcend the facile binary of good and evil are effectively silenced. Dogmatic ideology brutalizes the men and women who do not order their lives by its creeds. Those who inhabit the incommensurable universes of the True Islam, the True Christianity, the True Judaism of the Chosen People, believe in their Truths with absolute certainty. The result is a world of threat and obedience: a world that cannot recognize the actual complexities, inconvenient exceptions, partial solutions, and humble compromises of political reform.

Bush's War on Terror, with all its Orwellian rhetoric of "fighting for peace" and "killing to save lives," has moved the Muslim world away from the real possibility of democracy in two ways. It has given those who it had intended to obliterate new authority to represent the legitimate grievances of Muslims around the world. And, equally disturbing, it has generated a state of emergency within the Muslim world that marginalizes those involved in the painstaking work of social transformation. In a public sphere ringing with screaming choruses of indignation and grief, it is harder to focus on the long paragraphs and the complex sentences of political analysis and interpretation. The reformers in the Muslim world fight harder for an audience at home and are essentially eclipsed abroad.

Usama bin Laden's appearance in the days preceding the American election shows the consequence of a dogmatic rhetoric of good versus evil. Rather than representing himself as a terrorist on the run, bin Laden tried out the guise of a statesman with an agenda. He did not condemn Americans or Christians as infidels who deserve to be annihilated, nor did he intend to frighten Americans with his hatred. Rather, he conveyed a message of hope and resistance for Muslims. He carefully cataloged American policies in the Middle East and declared that "contrary to Bush's claim that we hate freedom," "we fight because we are free men who don't sleep under oppression." He condemned the Israeli invasion of Lebanon in 1982 and the ensuing massacres of Palestinian women and children in refugee camps. America had defended the legitimacy of Israel's atrocities. On that day, he intoned "it was confirmed to me that Destruction is freedom and democracy, while resistance is terrorism and intolerance."

This is a fabrication. Bin Laden is reinventing himself. In mid-1980s, after Israel's depredations in Lebanon, he was a young wealthy businessman with close ties to the Saudi royal family. He had found his religio-political calling in the mujahedin resistance to the Soviet occupation in Afghanistan, a joint operation of Reagan administration and the Pakistani intelligence services who created and recruited those "freedom fighters." When he joined them, bin Laden expressed no special sympathy with families of the massacred people in Beirut and Palestine. In his recent speech, bin Laden called his task of confronting the Bush administration difficult "in light of the resemblance it bears to the regimes in our countries, half of which are ruled by the military and the other half which are ruled by the sons of kings and presidents."[92] With his new rhetoric of social justice and anti-colonialism, he is clearly positioning himself as the heir to movements with whose founding ideas he had never identified.

The other political cost of the War on Terror is the effect of damping down voices of dissent within and outside Muslim countries. One of the first victims of this war was the Iranian reformist president Mohammad Khatami. President Bush's declaration of Iran as an axis of evil in his State of the Union address in 2002 was delivered at a moment when Islamic Republic had supported the American rout of the Taliban in Afghanistan. Iran had thrown its full support behind the transitional government of Hamid Karzai. But a reform movement in Iran cannot survive when the Administration continually waves the flag of regime change. The possibility of invasion offers

92 https://www.aljazeera.com/news/2004/11/1/full-transcript-of-bin-ladins-speech

existing regimes throughout the region the best tool to silence the opposition and treat them as agents of foreign powers. There were many institutional reasons for President Khatami's failure to realize his reformist agenda. But President Bush's messianic militarism does not leave much room for political actors such as the Iranian president to pursue the far more delicate business of creating an avenue for a rapprochement between political adversaries, for Khatami's humanistic dialogue of civilizations.

Bush's crusade obstructs genuine democratic reform that springs from Muslim societies. Rather, it equates reform with pro-Americanism, and therefore renders ineffective the political authority of reformists and obscures the role of those who wish to participate in their project. It inhibits those who engage Muslim societies critically to submit their critique freely without the fear of having their views misappropriated by apologists for Bush's War on Terror. Critical views will not flourish if they are to be used for justification of war.

The War on Terror replicates the logic of terrorism where intimidation and violence are considered to be the supremely effective means for political engagement. Both the War on Terror and terrorism eliminate the possibility of public participation. They repress the very people on behalf of whom they profess to speak. But Muslim societies will transform in spite of these doctrines, not because of them.

The global networks of terrorism and the administration's misguided policy against it together have substituted violence for critique, bullets for words, and destruction for change. The Polish social philosopher Zygmunt Bauman once wrote that in order to avert murder a human being needs to be augured towards words.[93] Peoples whose voices are heard and their grievances acknowledged will not resort to violence and will not submit to the authority of terrorists. Alas, the voice of this author will not be heard in the policy rooms of this Administration.

93 Zygmunt Bauman, *Postmodernity and Its Discontents,* New York: NYU Press, 1997.

25
Thomas Friedman's Muslim Problem

July 2005

In his op ed, "If It's a Muslim Problem, It Needs a Muslim Solution", in the July 8 edition of the New York Times, Tom Friedman called on Muslims around the world to condemn the violence committed under their name by al Qaeda jihadists. Friedman's call is based on two false assumptions. First, he alleges that "to this day – to this day – no major Muslim cleric or religious body has ever issued a fatwa condemning Osama bin Laden. For Mr. Friedman's information, hundreds of esteemed Muslim scholars and influential theologians have categorically condemned al Qaeda terrorism as un-Islamic. They have repeatedly questioned the authority of bin Laden in issuing fatwas and the legitimacy of his so-called *jihad*.

Yesterday in Tehran, the imam of Friday prayer, ayatollah Imami Kashani, also denounced the attacks in London as un-Islamic. In his sermon, he reiterated the Iranian Ministry of Foreign Affairs' denunciation of the bombings in London and proclaimed that "the killing of innocent men, women, young, and old is neither conscionable nor a virtuous human quality." "These terrorist acts," he decreed unequivocally, "are not Islamic, they are savagery."

The second false presupposition Mr. Friedman puts forward is that bin Ladenite jihadism is a Muslim problem that begs Muslim solutions. I wonder whether throughout the years that the IRA terrorized Britons in London any pundit ever called the predicament of the Irish a "Catholic problem with Catholic solutions." It is so convenient for Mr. Friedman to bury the historical facts of the emergence of al Qaeda with the aid and assistance of the Reagan administration and Pakistani intelligence services. The problem of violence wrapped in an Islamic cloak does not make it Muslims' problem. It is true that Islam, like any other religion, is understood in competing and at times contradictory ways. But each of these competing interpretations of Islam corresponds and reacts to particular situations in which Muslims find themselves. One cannot understand violent interpretations of jihad outside the violence to which Muslim majority nations have been subjected. In other words, Islam is not innately predisposed to violence; it does not breed savagery ex nihilo, thus the fallacy of terrorism as a "Muslim problem." Somehow it is easier for many Western pundits to understand that rather than a "Catholic problem," violence in Northern Ireland had much to do with British Empire.

Mr. Friedman declares that "When jihadist-style bombings happen in Riyadh, that is a Muslim-Muslim problem. That is a police problem for Saudi Arabia. But when Al-Qaeda-like bombings come to the London Underground, that becomes a civilizational problem." Then he rushes to position himself as a defender of Muslims' rights in the West by observing that these attacks would harm their civil liberties and will turn each Muslim into a suspect. With friends like Tom, who needs enemies! As a zealous advocate of unregulated globalization, Mr. Friedman ought to know that jihadists fighting the Saudi police on the streets of Riyadh is hardly an internal matter of Saudi Arabia. Fighting a police force that is trained by American advisors, armed by American-made weapons to protect the interests of an oppressive Royal Family supported by the US is far from a mere domestic dispute. What Mr. Friedman wants is a war away from home, where the casualties are unknown and the costs hidden.

"Jihadist-style bombings," in London, Madrid, and any other European or American cities are not inherently different from the same kinds of attacks on civilians in Baghdad, Tehran, Bali, Riyadh, or anywhere else in the Muslim world. They are neither civilizational nor do they have anything to do with Islam. An al-Qaeda attack on innocent civilians is as much part of Islam as Timothy McVeigh was a descendant of Thomas Jefferson. Mr. Friedman declares that "The double-decker buses of London and the subways of Paris, as well as the covered markets of Riyadh, Bali and Cairo, will never be secure as long as the Muslim village and elders do not take on, delegitimize, condemn and isolate the extremists in their midst."

Mr. Friedman's prescription hides the historical and political roots of terrorism. It does not matter what the Saudis teach in their primary and secondary schools about Christians and Jews so long as every Saudi citizen understands which world powers support their corrupt regime, which countries seal their mouth against injustices in their country to keep open the flow of oil. It does not matter how much the "Muslim village and elders" condemn bin Ladenites, so long as the US government continues to support tyrannical regimes of Central Asia, and builds military bases on soils tainted by the blood of innocent people. A just solution to the plight of Palestinians and the end of Israeli occupation of their land contains terrorism more effectively than hundred decrees against violence and the promotion of the peaceful nature of jihad. These murderous atrocities are perpetuated only by the global network of terrorism and the warmongering Anglo-American administrations who have substituted violence for critique, bullets for words, destruction for change, and occupation for liberation.

26

When a Cartoon Is Not a Cartoon: *What is funny about a demonized prophet?**

February 2006

**Including these cartoons in this piece might raise a question about the wisdom of their reproduction here. Although I consider all these images to be offensive, I believe it is imperative to feature those images for analytical purposes.*

Last September *Jyllands-Posten*, a Danish conservative daily, published twelve cartoons of Prophet Muhammad.[94] The cartoons were the paper's response to a Danish author's complaint that he could not find an artist who would be willing to draw illustrations for a book on the life of Prophet Mohammad. The paper ran twelve cartoons, in all of which the Prophet was depicted in

94 https://www.brusselsjournal.com/node/698

derogatory ways. One cartoonist portrayed him as an apparent terrorist with a bomb-shaped turban, and in another he appears above the clouds warning the apparent martyrs that heaven had ran out of virgins.

Three weeks ago, the cartoons were reprinted in *Magazinet,* a Christian evangelical newspaper in Norway, but later the newspaper decided to withdraw the cartoon from its website in the face of death threats.[95] While the first run of the cartoons sparked some protest in Denmark, the reprints generated intense outrage in Muslim communities around Europe, and in the last few days, in many

95 https://www.mediawatchwatch.org.uk/2006/01/16/magazinet-withdraws-mohammed-cartoons/

Muslim countries. Muslim groups in Europe and in the Middle East have called for a boycott of Danish products and have demanded an apology from the offending newspapers. The protests that began as peaceful condemnation has now turned violent and has escalated into an international crisis.

One of the cartoons, drawn by Lars Refn, prophesized the "seriousness of the Muslim threat to free speech." Refn drew a student named Mohammad in front of a chalkboard on which is written in Farsi "Jyllands-Posten's journalists are all reactionary provocateurs." The paper apologized for offending Muslims but maintains that "the 12 drawings were sober. They were not intended to be offensive, nor were they at variance with Danish law, but they have indisputably offended many Muslims for which we apologize."

But now Jyllands-Posten's apology and the Danish government's damage-control efforts are becoming irrelevant, as other European papers and governments, led by the French in their assiduous thirst for freedom, have come once again to the defense of freedom of speech. On Wednesday, February 1, *France Soir* published the twelve original cartoons and added an additional one in which Buddhist, Jewish, Christian holy figures console the Muslim Prophet, "Don't worry Muhammad, we've all been caricatured here."

France soir

Les Bronzés 3, c'est parti !

Pages 2-3

Dernière édition 0,90 €

Mercredi 1er février 2006

Oui, on a le droit de caricaturer Dieu

La parution de douze dessins dans la presse danoise a provoqué l'émotion du monde musulman pour qui la représentation d'Allah et de son prophète est interdite. Mais parce que nul dogme religieux ne peut s'imposer à une société démocratique et laïque, *France Soir* publie les caricatures incriminées

Publications in Germany, Spain, Italy, and the Netherlands have all reprinted these cartoons in support of free speech. One Dutch commentator observed, "we fought for freedom of religion and we need to defend it!"

While most pundits have tried to sell the case as a high-minded defense of free expression, I don't buy it! At what point does an expression transgress the boundaries of decency and become hate-speech, and therefore not protected by laws or basic principles of freedom?

Denmark is home to more than 200,000 Muslim immigrants whose very presence in Danish society has fueled anti-immigrant sentiments. This of course is not a Danish problem.

Rather than a sudden urge to defend the freedom of religion, the reprinting of the cartoons by many newspapers in different parts of Europe suggests that the Danes are not alone in their disdain of their Muslim minorities.

The Europeans share a skepticism that Muslims have no intention of assimilating into their societies and will exploit the generous European systems of social support without sharing the social values that come with it. In my opinion, the cartoons are not about Islam or the Prophet Muhammad. They are about Muslims whose presence disturbs European notions of the political, cultural, and aesthetic order.

Admittedly, a fine line separates hate-speech from free speech. This line becomes thinner when the speech is expressed in cartoons or other forms of visual art. Controversies arise when symbols and signs are used to humiliate a group of people who have been degraded and dehumanized in the past, or do not presently have the same means and powers to disseminate their own symbolic language. A cartoon ceases to be comic if the same groups of people who find that cartoon amusing have violated the dignity of its subject.

Western societies typically uphold the belief that expressions which incite violence and are generally regarded as demagogic, should not enjoy legal and political protection.

We have many examples of these ugly and degrading racial expressions in American society that ended only after decades of struggle and protest. I have no doubt that no one would think twice about suppressing reprints of Nazi anti-Semitic propaganda in American or European papers. Indeed, in June 2003, responding to pressures from several prominent Jewish groups, the Chicago Tribune issued an official apology for printing an offensive cartoon by Dick Locher. It depicted a hook-nosed figure of Ariel Sharon gazing at rows of dollar bills that President Bush is carefully laying down across a bridge called "MIDEAST GULCH."

The Sharon figure exclaims, "On second thought, the pathway to peace is looking a bit brighter." The confident Yasser Arafat awaits him on the other side. It is not hard to see the anti-Semitic insinuation of the cartoon, as it invokes a stereotypical portrayal of "the avaricious Jew" who would do any deed for money. Anything that resembles Nazi propaganda rightfully generates anxiety and anger among Jewish people. There is no satire in cartoons which remind us how historic degradation of European Jews justified their massacre.

„Der Gott des Juden ist das Geld. Und um Geld zu verdienen, begeht er die größten Verbrechen. Er ruht nicht eher, bis er auf einem großen Geldsack sitzen kann, bis er zum König des Geldes geworden ist."

Ernst Hiemer, "The God of the Jews Is Money," 1938.
See "Caricature or Bigotry?"[96]

96 https://www.camera.org/article/caricature-or-bigotry/

The Chicago Tribune had to apologize, and it did. And no one accused Jewish groups who demanded an apology of intolerance. Nobody declared that Jewish groups did not respect the freedom of expression. Not a single newspaper in Europe or North America would reprint a Nazi cartoon with a caption that reads: "The God of the Jew is Money. And to gain money, he will commit the greatest crimes..." They should not, because this is not a matter of free expression.

To give another example, when in 1993, the American actor Ted Danson appeared in black face at a Friars Club roast of the actress Whoopi Goldberg, there was an outcry in the black community about his insensitivity to the history of black oppression and how minstrel acts intended to dehumanize blacks. The Friars Club apologized, and Danson suffered career setbacks for his poor judgment.

Another example of demagogic expressions and demands for apology: Today there is an ongoing struggle over the usage of Native American mascots for American sports teams. The imagery and actions associated with these mascots reinforce stereotypes of indigenous peoples as "demonic," "aggressive," and "warmongering." They turn the image of a native warrior into a savage caricature.

Mascots turn people into mere historical objects without contemporary relevance. The supporters argue that mascots entertain audiences and should not become the subject of political debates and historical investigation. Fun is fun and by definition should not be taken seriously. For native peoples who were prohibited by Europeans from performing their own rituals in public, seeing whites dancing with colored faces and heads decorated with eagle feathers does not evoke humor or entertainment.

As one Native American leader commented: "We experience [the use of Native mascots] as no less than a mockery of our cultures. We see objects sacred to us - such as eagle feathers, face painting and traditional dress - being used not in sacred ceremony, or in any cultural setting, but in another culture's game... Yes, we are proud of the warriors who fought to protect our cultures from forced removal and systematic genocide and to preserve our lands from the greed of others. We are proud, and we don't want them demeaned by being "honored" in a sports activity on a playing field."

That was why in April 2003, the US Commission on Civil Rights called on school and professional sports teams to eliminate all derogatory symbols that trivialize Native American religions and cultures.

The case of the cartoons of the Prophet Muhammad is no exception to the public recognition of the difference between freedom of expression and hate-speech. What is considered to be demagogic and what is satirical, what is regarded as degrading and what is entertainment, what expressions ought to be prohibited and what is permissible are political questions with historically specific answers.

Those in Europe who think that they need to fight a battle for free speech and freedom of religion need to think harder and more reflexively about whose war they are fighting and who their enemies are. A bomb-turbaned Prophet turns all Muslims into terrorists. One must be free to satirize suicide bombers or terrorists of any persuasion. But lampooning Islam as *inherently* intolerant and Muslims as terrorist is neither wise nor commendable. In the American context, no one would call the spectacle of whites mocking blacks humorous.

Muslims who turn to violence in order to register their displeasure with the cartoons only turn themselves into the same caricatures against which they protest. Demanding an apology or boycotting consumer products are legitimate means of expression so long as they do not trade in words for bullets. Fists are the strongest when they are waved in the air, not when they land on the opponent's face.

Instead of congratulating themselves for upholding the fine tradition of the freedom of speech, and savoring their prophesy of "Muslim Rage," the French, British, Germans, Dutch, and Belgians shall recall Algeria, India, the Congo, and Indonesia. The *Jyllands-Posten* scandal is not about a cartoon, it is rather a reminder of a postcolonial world that has not yet come to terms with its own past.

Acknowledgements

We live in scary and unpredictable times. From the domestic politics in the US and its extortionist imperialism around the world, to the planetary perils of our ecosystem, every single day we hear and see things that just a few months ago seemed inconceivable. By the time this book is published its significance might have already melted into air. But I offer these interventions to remind us that the emergence of this condition was never inevitable. Political decisions were made, economic policies implemented, wars inaugurated, injustices levied, and policies instituted that have led to what we witness today. This book is a small reminder of who the decision-makers were and how those voices of justice were marginalized in one beloved corner of this unsettled world.

This book comprises more than twenty years of writing on Iran-US relations and their respective domestic politics. The list of those from whose ideas and thoughts I have benefitted is long. Authorship is a communal work, and I have been extremely fortunate that my community is broad and brilliant. Through these years I have been endowed with the support of friends and colleagues who have contributed to my intellectual and personal growth. Now that I have retired, I feel that privilege more perceptibly. My colleagues and friends at Georgia State University in Atlanta (1999-2005), Wendy Simonds, Chip Gallagher, and Jung-Ha Kim; at the University of Illinois (2005-2019), Tariq Ali, Clare Crowston, Dave Roediger, Teresa Barnes, James Kilgore, Tamara Chaplin, Erik McDuffie, Peter Fritzsche, Carol Symes, Marc Hertzman, Mauro Nobili, Bruce Levine, Michale Rothberg, Yasemin Yildiz; and at Princeton (2019-2025), Max Weiss, Lara Harb, Julia Elyachar, Dan Sheffield, Zia Mian, Zahid Chaudhuri, Carolyn Rouse, Razia Iqbal, and all the postdoctoral fellows at the Iran Center.

Many people have left a lasting mark on my writing. I am certain that I am going to fail mentioning them all. Antoinette Burton, Niloofar Haeri, Zohreh Sullivan, Faranak Miraftab, Manuel Rota, Nora Stoppino, Maria Todorova, Zsuzsa Gille, Asef Bayat, Linda Herrera, Arzoo Osanloo, Minoo Moallem, Saba Mahmood, Joan Scott, Susan Buck-Morss, Elias Khoury, Babak Rahimi, Naghmeh Sohrabi, Nasrin Rahimieh, Asad Kabir, Fereshteh Ahmadi, Tera Hunter, Siavash Saffari, Arash Davari, Narges Bajoghli, Golnar Nikpour, Donna Honarpisheh, Banu Bargu, Mohamad Tavakoli, Milad Odabaei, Naveed Mansoori, Ladan Heravi, Abbas Jong, Veneta Ivanova, Heba Khalil, Eva Rogaar, Fadi Bardawil, Tony Alessandrini, Leila Pourtavaf, and Usha and Rajmohan Gandhi. From early on in my academic pursuit, I was inspired by Talal Asad's ideas. His influence on my thinking only grew as we cultivated a friendship, which I deeply cherish. My precious New York community, Herman Bennett, Jennifer Morgan, Thuy Linh Tu, Nikhil Singh, Gary Wilder, Miriam Ticktin, Mana Kia, and Andrew Ross helped me to find solid ground during hard times when I needed to reorient myself and find my compass again. Sharon Ghamari-Tabrizi has always offered sound critique and editorial comments, especially on earlier essays, for that and her friendship I am most grateful.

I could not exist in this world without selfless support and encouragement of my family, my late parents and my sister Behjat and brothers Bijan and Behdad, my nieces Donya and Mana, my partner Julie and step-daughter Hazel. Julie Livingston has shown me that the world starts from home. Everything we utter about the world needs to find its reflection at home, and vice-versa. She has been a teacher in generosity, offering unaffected love and intellectual oomph without measure.

Finally, special thanks for Jeffrey St Clair for years of support and encouragement, Colin Robinson and the OR Books team, Olivia, Zahra, and those behind the scenes.

Photo by Nancy Castro

Behrooz Ghamari is affiliated with the Elahé Omidyar Mir-Djalali Institute of Iranian Studies at the University of Toronto. He was Professor and Chair of the Department of Near Eastern Studies and Director of the Center for Iran and Persian Gulf Studies at Princeton University from 2020 to 2024. He is the author of three books on different aspects and historical context of the Iranian revolution of 1979 and its aftermath: *Islam and Dissent in Post-Revolutionary Iran* (2008); *Foucault in Iran: Islamic Revolution after the Enlightenment* (2016); and *Remembering Akbar: Inside the Iranian Revolution,* OR Books (2016).

www.ingramcontent.com/pod-product-compliance
Lightning Source LLC
Jackson TN
JSHW031739250626
104373JS00001B/2
9781682196717